S0-BLS-696

Filipino (Tagalog)
Phrase Book
&
Dictionary

Berlitz Publishing

New York   Munich   Singapore

Contacting the Editors
Every effort has been made to provide accurate information in this publication, but changes are inevitable. The publisher cannot be responsible for any resulting loss, inconvenience or injury. We would appreciate it if readers would call our attention to any errors or outdated information. We also welcome your suggestions; if you come across a relevant expression not in our phrase book, please contact us: comments@berlitzpublishing.com

Printed in China by CTPS, December 2010

Publishing Director: Sheryl Olinsky Borg
Senior Editor/Project Manager: Lorraine Sova
Translation: Datagrafix, Inc.
Cover Design: Claudia Petrilli
Interior Design: Derrick Lim, Juergen Bartz
Production Manager: Elizabeth Gaynor
Cover Photo: © Steve Vidler/SuperStock
Interior Photos: p. 13 © H.W.A.C; p. 18 © David Guyler/2007 iStock International Inc.;
p. 28 © Pixtal/ Agefotostock; p. 42 © Corbis/fotosearch.com; p. 55 © Ryan McVay/Photodisc/
Agefotostock; p. 61 © Sarah Encabo/flickr.com; p. 63 © Stockbyte Photography/2002 – 07 Veer
Incorporated; p. 77 © Lorelyn Medina/2003 – 2007 Shutterstock, Inc.; p. 85 © ImageDJ/Alamy; p. 90
© Netfalls/2003 – 2007 Shutterstock, Inc.; p. 107 © Marcus Brown/2007 iStock International Inc.;
p. 111 © BananaStock Ltd.; p. 117 © Daniel Thistlethwaite/PictureQuest; p. 119 © Daniel
Gustavsson/2003 – 2007 Shutterstock, Inc.; p. 123 © laszlo a. lim/2003 – 2007 Shutterstock, Inc.; p. 126
© 2007 Jupiterimages Corporation; p. 136 © eric florentin/2003 – 2007 Shutterstock, Inc.; p. 152
© Jupiterimages/Brand X/Corbis; p. 154 © Stockbyte/Fotosearch.com; p. 157 © Corbis/2006
JupiterImages Corporation; p. 161 © David McKee/2003 – 2007 Shutterstock, Inc.; p. 162, 167
© 2007 Jupiterimages Corporation

Distribution
UK & Ireland: GeoCenter International Ltd., Meridian House, Churchill Way West,
Basingstoke, Hampshire RG21 6YR. email: sales@geocenter.co.uk

United States: Ingram Publisher Services, One Ingram Boulevard, PO Box 3006,
La Vergne, TN 37086-1986. email: customer.service@ingrampublisherservices.com

Worldwide: Apa Publications GmbH & Co., Verlag KG (Singapore branch), 7030
Ang Mo Kio Avenue 5, 08-65 Northstar @ AMK, Singapore 569880
email: apasin@singnet.com.sg

Contents

Survival

Food

People

Special Needs

Resources

Dictionary

How to Use This Book

These essential phrases can also be heard on the audio CD.

Sometimes you see two alternatives in italics, separated by a slash. Choose the one that's right for your situation.

Essential

I'm on *vacation [holiday]/business*.	***Nakabakasyón/On official business* akó.** nah·kah·bah·kah·*shohn*/ohn oh·*fee*·syal *bees*·nehs ah·*koh*
I'm going to…	**Púpunta akó sa…** poo·poon·tah ah·*koh* sah…
I'm staying at the… Hotel.	**Tumútulóy akó sa…Hotél.** too·moo·too·*lohy* ah·*koh* sah…hoh·*tehl*

You May See...

CÚSTOMS	customs
DÚTY-FREE GOODS	duty-free goods
GOODS NA IDEDEKLARÁ	goods to declare

ATM, Bank and Currency Exchange

I'd like to…	**Gustó kong…** goos·*toh* kohng…
– change money	**– magpápalít ng péra** mahg·*pah*·pah·*leet* nahng peh·rah
– change *dollars/ pounds* into pesos	**– magpápalít ng *dóllars/pounds* sa píso** mahg·*pah*·pah·*leet* nahng *dah*·lahrs/pahwnds sah *pee*·soh
– cash *traveler's checks [cheques]/*	**– magpápalít ng *tráveler's checks/ Eúrochecks*	

Words you may see are shown in *You May See* boxes.

Any of the words or phrases preceded by dashes can be plugged into the sentence above.

Filipino phrases appear in red.

Read the simplified pronunciation as if it were Filipino. For more on pronunciation, see page 10.

Relationships

I'm...	**...akó.** ...ah·<u>koh</u>
– single	– **Binatà** ♂/**Dalága** ♀ bee·<u>nah</u>·tah' ♂/ dah·<u>lah</u>·gah ♀
– in a relationship	– **May bóyfrien**~~d~~ bohy·frehnd ♂/ge
– engaged/married	– **Ikákasal na/M** ee·<u>kah</u>·kah·sahl
– divorced	– **Diborsyádo** ♂/**Diborsyáda** ♀ dee·bohr·<u>shah</u>·doh ♂/dee·bohr·<u>shah</u>·dah ♀

When different gender forms apply, the masculine form is followed by ♂; feminine by ♀.

▶ For Filipino pronouns, see page 177.

The arrow indicates a cross reference where you'll find related phrases.

Information boxes contain relevant country, culture and language tips.

 A handshake is a common business greeting for both men and women. English is widely used in government and business sectors and, so, English greetings may be used.

You May Hear...

Méron ba kayóng appóintment?
<u>meh</u>·rohn bah kah·<u>yohng</u> ah·<u>pohynt</u>·mehnt

Kaníno? kah·<u>nee</u>·noh

Do you have an appointment?

With whom?

Expressions you may hear are shown in *You May Hear* boxes.

Color-coded side bars identify each section of the book.

9

Pronunciation

This section is designed to make you familiar with the sounds of Filipino using our simplified phonetic transcription. You'll find the pronunciation of the Filipino letters and sounds explained below, together with their "imitated" equivalents. This system is used throughout the phrase book; simply read the pronunciation as if it were English, noting any special rules below.

Generally, Filipino is a phonetic language—there is a good correlation of sound to spelling. Underlined letters indicate that that syllable should be stressed. Unlike English, stress in Filipino is not nearly so strong. Generally, it sounds as though all syllables are given equal value, except when the syllable is marked with the following:

- The **pahilís** (acute accent) (´) indicates that the syllable is stressed more than others.

- The **pakupyâ** (circumflex accent) (^), which may appear on a vowel at the end of a word, indicates that the syllable is stressed and ends with a short burst of air (that is, a glottal stop). A glottal stop is represented in this phrase book by '.

You may also see a vowel at the end of a word with the **paiwa** (grave accent) (`). This indicates that the last syllable should end with a short burst of air (glottal stop).

A word without an accent is automatically stressed on the penultimate syllable (that is, the second to last syllable).

Stress in Filipino is of utmost importance—it is not only a guide to pronunciation but also determines meaning. For example:

áso (dog)	[<u>ah</u>-soh]
asó (smoke)	[ah-<u>soh</u>]

Written materials in Filipino generally do not show accent marks; exceptions include Filipino dictionaries and usage guides. Throughout this phrase book, accents are shown to help establish correct speech patterns and distinguish between words that have the same spelling but different meanings.

Consonants

Letter	Approximate Pronunciation	Symbol	Example	Pronunciation
c	1. when followed by consonants and a, o and u, like c in cat	k	**café**	kah·<u>fehy</u>
	2. when followed by h, like ch in check	ch	**lechón**	leh·<u>chon</u>
	3. when followed by e or i, like s in safe	s	**tocíno**	toh·<u>see</u>·noh
d	1. as in English	d	**dalawá**	dah·lah·<u>wah</u>
	2. when followed by y and a vowel, like j in juice	j	**dyáryo**	<u>jahr</u>·yoh
j	1. as in English	j	**juice**	joos
	2. in some Spanish-derived words and proper nouns, like h in hat	h	**júsi**	<u>hoo</u>·see
l	1. as in English	l	**labás**	lah·<u>bahs</u>
	2. in borrowed Spanish words with a double l sequence, the l sound is followed by a y sound	ly	**pastíllas**	pahs·<u>teel</u>·yahs
ng	like ng in sing	ng	**ngayón**	ngah·<u>yohn</u>
r	as in English, but rolled	r	**rádyo**	<u>rah</u>·joh

s	1. like s in safe	s	**silángan**	see·<u>lah</u>·ngahn
	2. when followed by y and a vowel, like sh in shampoo	sh	**présyo**	<u>preh</u>·shoh
t	1. like t in stop	t	**tátay**	<u>tah</u>·tahy
	2. when followed by s and a vowel, like ch in check	ch	**tsaá**	chah·<u>ah</u>

Letters b, f, g, h, k, m, n, p, q, v, w, x, y and z are pronounced as in English.

Vowels

Letter	Approximate Pronunciation	Symbol	Example	Pronunciation
a	like a in father	ah	**akó**	ah·<u>koh</u>
e	like e in bed	eh	**edukádo**	eh·doo·<u>kah</u>·doh
i	like ee in feet	ee	**inosénte**	ee·noh·<u>sehn</u>·teh
o	like o in or	oh	**óras**	<u>oh</u>·rahs
u	like u in rule	oo	**útos**	<u>oo</u>·tohs

Filipino is the national language of the Philippines, though various dialects and provincial languages are spoken in the country as well. Filipino is currently undergoing modernization; the Manila dialect of the Filipino, known as Tagalog, is the *lingua franca.* This phrase book and dictionary presents the Metro Manila Filipino language.

English is also an official language of the Philippines.

Luzon Str.
Babuyan Is.

on ●Baguio
Dagupan ●
Mt. Pinatubo ●Cabanatuan
Angeles ● Quezon City
MANILA ● Lucena
Batangas ● ● Naga
Mindoro
PHILIPPINES
Calamian Group ● *Panay* *Samar*
Iloilo● ● Tacloban
Palawan Bacolod● ●Cebu
Negros
Sulu Sea Iligan● ●Butuan
Pagadian● ● Cagayan de Oro
Balabac I. Zamboanga● *Mindanao*
Jolo● Davao●
MALAYSIA General Santos
Sulu Arch. *Celebes* *Talaud Is.*
Sea

PHILIP
SE

▼ *Survival*

Arrival and Departure

Essential

I'm on *vacation* [*holiday*]/business.	**Nakabakasyón/On official búsiness akó.** nah·kah·bah·kah·<u>shohn</u>/ohn oh·<u>fee</u>·shal <u>bees</u>·nehs ah·<u>koh</u>
I'm going to…	**Púpunta akó sa…** poo·poon·<u>tah</u> ah·<u>koh</u> sah…
I'm staying at the… Hotel.	**Tumútulóy akó sa…Hotél.** too·moo·too·<u>lohy</u> ah·<u>koh</u> sah…hoh·<u>tehl</u>

You May Hear…

Ang pasapórte ninyó, please. ahng pah·sah·<u>pohr</u>·teh neen·<u>yoh</u> plees	Your passport, please.
Anó ang dahilán ng inyóng pagbisíta? ah·<u>noh</u> ahng dah·hee·<u>lahn</u> nahng een·<u>yohng</u> pahg·bee·<u>see</u>·tah	What's the purpose of your visit?
Saán kayó tumútulóy? sah·<u>ahn</u> kah·<u>yoh</u> too·<u>moo</u>·too·<u>lohy</u>	Where are you staying?
Gaáno kayó katagál díto? gah·<u>ah</u>·noh kah·<u>yoh</u> kah·tah·<u>gahl</u> dee·toh	How long are you staying?
Síno ang kasáma mo díto? <u>see</u>·noh ahng kah·<u>sah</u>·mah moh <u>dee</u>·toh	Who are you here with?

Passport Control and Customs ───

I'm just passing through.	**Napadaán lang akó.** nah·pah·dah·<u>ahn</u> lahng ah·<u>koh</u>

I'm on my own.	**Mag-isá lang akó.**	mahg·ee·<u>sah</u> lahng ah·<u>koh</u>
I'm with my family.	**Kasáma ko ang áking pamílya.**	kah·<u>sah</u>·mah koh ahng <u>ah</u>·keeng pah·<u>meel</u>·yah
I'm with a group.	**Kasáma ko ang isáng grúpo.**	kah·<u>sah</u>·mah koh ahng ee·<u>sahng</u> <u>groo</u>·poh
I'd like to declare…	**Gustó kong ideklará…**	goos·<u>toh</u> kohng ee·dehk·lah·<u>rah</u>…
I have nothing to declare.	**Walâ akóng idedeklará.**	wah·<u>lah</u>' ah·<u>kohng</u> ee·deh·dehk·lah·<u>rah</u>

You May Hear...

Méron ba kayóng idedeklará? <u>meh</u>·rohn bah kah·<u>yohng</u> ee·deh·dehk·lah·<u>rah</u>	Anything to declare?
Kailángan ninyóng magbáyad ng buwís díto. kah·ee·<u>lah</u>·ngahn neen·<u>yohng</u> mahg·<u>bah</u>·yahd nahng boo·<u>wees</u> <u>dee</u>·toh	You must pay duty on this.

You May See...

CÚSTOMS	customs
DÚTY-FREE GOODS	duty-free goods
GOODS NA IDEDEKLARÁ	goods to declare
WALÁNG IDEDEKLARÁ	nothing to declare
KONTRÓL NG PASAPÓRTE	passport control
PULÍS	police

Money and Banking

Essential

Where's...?	**Saán...?** sah-<u>ahn</u>...
– the ATM	**– ang ATM** ahng ehy-tee-ehm
– the bank	**– ang bángko** ahng <u>bahng</u>-koh
– the currency exchange office	**– ang pálitan ng péra** ahng <u>pah</u>-lee-tahn nahng <u>peh</u>-rah
When does the bank *open/close*?	**Kailán *nagbubukás/nagsasará* ang bángko?** kah-ee-<u>lahn</u> *nahg-boo-boo-<u>kahs</u>/ nahg-sah-sah-<u>rah</u>* ahng <u>bahng</u>-koh
I'd like to change *dollars/pounds* into pesos.	**Gustó kong magpápalít ng *dóllars/ pounds* sa píso.** goos-<u>toh</u> kohng mahg-<u>pah</u>-pah-<u>leet</u> nahng *<u>dah</u>-lahrs/pahwnds* sah <u>pee</u>-soh
I'd like to cash traveler's checks [cheques].	**Gustó kong magpápalít ng tráveler's checks.** goos-<u>toh</u> kohng mahg-<u>pah</u>-pah-<u>leet</u> nahng <u>trah</u>-veh-lehrs chehks

ATM, Bank and Currency Exchange

I'd like to...	**Gustó kong...** goos-<u>toh</u> kohng...
– change money	**– magpápalít ng péra** mahg-<u>pah</u>-pah-<u>leet</u> nahng <u>peh</u>-rah
– change *dollars/ pounds* into pesos	**– magpápalít ng *dóllars/pounds* sa píso** mahg-<u>pah</u>-pah-<u>leet</u> nahng *<u>dah</u>-lahrs/pahwnds* sah <u>pee</u>-soh
– cash *traveler's checks [cheques]/ Eurocheques*	**– magpápalít ng *tráveler's checks/ Eúrochecks*** mahg-<u>pah</u>-pah-<u>leet</u> nahng *<u>trah</u>-veh-lehrs checks/<u>yoo</u>-roh-chehks*
– get a cash advance	**– bumále** boo-<u>mah</u>-leh

What's the exchange rate?	**Anó ba ang pálitan?** ah-<u>noh</u> bah ahng <u>pah</u>-lee-tahn
I think there's a mistake.	**Sa palagáy ko may malî.** sah pah-lah-<u>gahy</u> koh mahy mah-<u>lee</u>'
I lost my traveler's checks [cheques].	**Nawalâ ang tráveler's checks ko.** nah-wah-<u>lah</u>' ahng <u>trah</u>-veh-lehrs chehks koh
My card...	**...ang card ko.** ...ahng kahrd koh
– was lost	**– Nawalâ** nah-wah-<u>lah</u>'
– was stolen	**– Nanákaw** nah-<u>nah</u>-kahw
– doesn't work	**– Hindî gumagána** heen-<u>dee</u>' goo-mah-<u>gah</u>-nah

▶For numbers, see page 181.

ATMs are common throughout the Philippines and can be easily found in nearly every major city and medium-sized town; directions in English are available on all machines. Most ATMs accept Visa, Mastercard, Eurocard and other cards using the Plus and Cirrus systems. Some machines will take only local cards, while others can transact internationally; look at the signs on the machine to determine if your card will work. Transaction fees using overseas ATM cards can be high; check with your bank before leaving home. Debit cards are widely accepted too.

You May Hear...

Pwéde bang makíta ang inyóng *pasapórte/ID*? <u>pweh</u>·deh bahng mah·<u>kee</u>·tah ahng een·<u>yohng</u> *pah·sah·<u>pohr</u>·teh/<u>ahy</u>·dee*

Could I see your *passport/ID*?

Anó ang inyóng nasyonalidád? ah·<u>noh</u> ahng een·<u>yohng</u> nah·shoh·nah·lee·<u>dahd</u>

What's your nationality?

Saán ba kayó tumútulóy? sah·<u>ahn</u> bah kah·<u>yoh</u> too·<u>moo</u>·too·<u>lohy</u>

Where are you staying?

Méron ba kayóng ibáng ID? <u>meh</u>·rohn bah kah·<u>yohng</u> ee·<u>bahng</u> <u>ahy</u>·dee

Do you have other ID?

Sagután ang form na itó. sah·goo·<u>tahn</u> ahng fohrm nah ee·<u>toh</u>

Fill out this form.

Pakipirmahán díto. pah·kee·peer·mah·<u>hahn</u> <u>dee</u>·toh

Please sign here.

You May See...

Filipino currency is the **píso**, ₱, divided into 100 **centavos**.

Notes: 20, 50, 100, 200, 500 and 1000 pesos

Coins: 1, 5, 10 and 25 cents, 1, 5 and 10 pesos

Transportation

Essential

How do I get to town?	**Paáno ba akó makákapúnta sa báyan?** pah·ah·noh bah ah·koh mah·kah·kah·poon·tah sah bah·yahn
Where's…?	**Saán…?** sah·ahn…
– the airport	**– ang airport** ahng ehyr·pohrt
– the train [railway] station	**– ang estasyón ng tren** ahng ehs·tah·shohn nahng trehn
– the bus station	**– ang estasyón ng bus** ahng ehs·tah·shohn nahng boos
How far is it?	**Gaáno kalayò iyón?** gah·ah·noh kah·lah·yoh' ee·yohn
Where do I buy a ticket?	**Saán akó makákabilí ng tíket?** sah·ahn ah·koh mah·kah·kah·bee·lee nahng tee·keht
A *one-way/round-trip [return]* ticket to…	**Isáng *one-way/round-trip* tíket sa…** ee·sahng *wahn·wehy/rahwnd·treep* tee·keht sah…
How much?	**Magkáno?** mahg·kah·noh
Is there a discount?	**Méron bang diskwénto?** meh·rohn bahng dees·kwehn·toh
Which…?	**Alíng…?** ah·leeng…
– gate	**– gate** gehyt
– line	**– línya** leen·yah
– platform	**– plátform** plaht·fohrm
Where can I get a taxi?	**Saán akó pwédeng kumúha ng táksi?** sah·ahn ah·koh pweh·dehng koo·moo·hah nahng tahk·see

Take me to this address.	**Ihatíd mo akó sa adrés na itó.** ee·hah·<u>teed</u> moh ah·<u>koh</u> sah ahd·<u>rehs</u> nah ee·<u>toh</u>
Where's the car rental [hire]?	**Saán ang rentáhan ng sasakyán?** sah·<u>ahn</u> ahng rehn·<u>tah</u>·hahn nahng sah·sahk·<u>yahn</u>
Can I have a map?	**Pwéde bang humingî ng mápa?** <u>pweh</u>·deh bahng hoo·mee·<u>ngee</u>' nahng <u>mah</u>·pah

Ticketing

When's the…to Manila?	**Kailán ang…pa-Mayníla?** kah·ee·<u>lahn</u> ahng…pah·mahy·<u>nee</u>·lah
– (first) bus	**– (únang) bus** (<u>oo</u>·nahng) boos
– (next) flight	**– (súsunod) na lipád** (<u>soo</u>·soo·nohd) nah lee·<u>pahd</u>
– (last) train	**– (hulíng) tren** (hoo·<u>leeng</u>) trehn
Is there…trip?	**Méron bang biyáhe…?** <u>meh</u>·rohn bahng bee·<u>yah</u>·heh…
– an earlier	**– na mas maága** nah mahs mah·<u>ah</u>·gah
– a later	**– mamayâ** mah·mah·<u>yah</u>'
– an overnight	**– na magdamágan** nah mahg·dah·<u>mah</u>·gahn
– a cheaper	**– na mas múra** nah mahs <u>moo</u>·rah
Where do I buy a ticket?	**Saán pwédeng bumilí ng tíket?** sah·<u>ahn</u> <u>pwe</u>·dehng boo·mee·<u>lee</u> nahng <u>tee</u>·keht
One/Two ticket(s), please.	**Isáng/Dalawáng tíket, please.** ee·<u>sahng</u>/ dah·lah·<u>wahng</u> <u>tee</u>·keht plees
For today/tomorrow.	**Pára ngayón/búkas.**<u>pah</u>·rah ngah·<u>yohn</u>/ <u>boo</u>·kahs

▶For days, see page 183.

▶For time, see page 183.

A…ticket.	…tíket. …<u>tee</u>·keht
– one-way	**– Óne-way na** <u>wahn</u>·wehy nah
– round-trip [return]	**– Round trip na** <u>rahwnd</u> treep nah
– first class	**– First class** feerst klahs
– business class	**– Búsiness class** <u>bees</u>·nehs klahs
– economy class	**– Ecónomy class** eh·<u>koh</u>·noh·mee klahs
– one-day	**– Pang-isáng áraw na** pahng·ee·<u>sahng</u> <u>ah</u>·rahw nah
– multiple-trip	**– Pang-múltiple trip na** pahng·<u>mohl</u>·tee·pohl treep nah
How much?	**Magkáno?** mahg·<u>kah</u>·noh
Is there… discount?	**Méron bang…diskwénto?** <u>meh</u>·rohn bahng…dees·<u>kwehn</u>·toh
– a child	**– pambatà na** pahm·<u>bah</u>·tah' nah
– a student	**– pang-estudyánte na** pahng·ehs·tood·<u>yahn</u>·teh nah
– a senior citizen	**– pangmatandâ na** pahng·mah·tahn·<u>dah</u>' nah
The *express/local bus/train*, please.	*Ékspres/lókal bus/tren*, **please.** <u>ehks</u>·prehs/<u>loh</u>·kahl boos/trehn plees
I have an e-ticket.	**Méron akóng e-tíket.** <u>meh</u>·rohn ah·<u>kohng</u> ee·<u>tee</u>·keht
Can I buy a ticket on the…?	**Pwéde ba akóng bumilí ng tíket sa…?** <u>pweh</u>·deh bah ah·<u>kohng</u> boo·mee·<u>lee</u> nahng <u>tee</u>·keht sah…
Do I have to stamp the ticket before boarding?	**Kailángan ko bang patatakán ang tíket bágo sumakáy?** kah·ee·<u>lah</u>·ngahn koh bahng pah·tah·tah·<u>kahn</u> ahng <u>tee</u>·keht <u>bah</u>·goh soo·mah·<u>kahy</u>
How long is this ticket valid?	**Hanggáng kailán magagámit ang tíket na itó?** hahng·<u>gahng</u> kah·ee·<u>lahn</u> mah·gah·<u>gah</u>·meet ahng <u>tee</u>·keht nah ee·<u>toh</u>

I'd like to…my reservation.	**Gustó kong…ang resérbasyón ko.** goos·<u>toh</u> kohng…ahng reh·<u>sehr</u>·bah·<u>shohn</u> koh
– cancel	– **kanselahín** kahn·seh·lah·<u>heen</u>
– change	– **palitán** pah·lee·<u>tahn</u>
– confirm	– **kumpirmahín** koom·peer·mah·<u>heen</u>

Plane

Getting to the Airport

How much is a taxi to the airport?	**Magkáno ang báyad sa táksi papuntáng aírport?** mahg·<u>kah</u>·noh ahng <u>bah</u>·yahd sah <u>tahk</u>·see pah·poon·<u>tahng</u> ehyr·pohrt
To…Airport, please.	**Sa…Airport, please.** sah…<u>ehyr</u>·pohrt plees
My airline is…	**Ang airline ko ay…** ang <u>ehyr</u>·lahyn koh ahy…
My flight leaves at…	**Ang flight ko ay áalis ng alás…** ahng flahyt koh ahy <u>ah</u>·ah·<u>lees</u> nahng ah·<u>lahs</u>…
I'm in a rush.	**Nagmamadalî akó.** nahg·mah·mah·dah·<u>lee</u>' ah·<u>koh</u>

▶For time, see page 183.

Can you drive *faster/slower*?	**Pwéde ba ninyóng *bilisán/bagálan* ang pag-drive?** <u>pweh</u>·deh bah neen·<u>yohng</u> *bee·lee·<u>sahn</u>/bah·<u>gah</u>·lahn* ahng pahg·<u>drahyv</u>

You May Hear…

Anóng airline ang inyóng sásakyan? ah·<u>nohng</u> <u>ehyr</u>·lahyn ahng een·<u>yohng</u> <u>sah</u>·sahk·yahn	What airline are you flying?
Doméstik o internásyonal? doh·<u>mehs</u>·teek oh een·tehr·<u>nah</u>·shoh·nahl	Domestic or international?
Anóng términál? ah·<u>nohng</u> <u>tehr</u>·mee·<u>nahl</u>	What terminal?

i Philippine Airlines (PAL) is the country's national carrier, with regular routes throughout Asia Pacific, to the United States and the Middle East. Together with its sister company, Air Philippines, PAL also flies to all major cities in the Philippines. The other major airline in the country is Cebu Pacific, a low-cost carrier, which flies throughout the Philippines and to several destinations in Asia.

Ninoy Aquino International Airport (NAIA) Terminal 1 in Parañaque City services most international flights, while nearby NAIA Terminal 2, the Centennial Terminal, services only PAL. Mactan International Airport in Cebu offers flights from many domestic and international carriers. Diosdado Macapagal International Airport at Clark Field, Pampanga, has recently become home to several low-cost regional carriers.

You May See...

PAGDATÍNG	arrivals
PAPAALÍS	departures
SEGURIDÁD	security
MGÁ BIYÁHENG DOMÉSTIK	domestic flights
MGÁ BIYÁHENG INTERNÁSYONAL	international flights
CHÉCK-IN	check-in
E-TÍCKET CHÉCK-IN	e-ticket check-in
DEPÁRTURE GATES	departure gates

Check-in and Boarding

Where's check-in?	**Saán ang chéck-in?**	sah-<u>ahn</u> ahng <u>chehk</u>-een
My name is…	**…ang pangálan ko.**	…ahng pah-<u>ngah</u>-lahn koh
I'm going to…	**Púpuntá akó sa…**	<u>poo</u>-poon-<u>tah</u> ah-<u>koh</u> sah…
I have…	**Méron akóng…**	<u>meh</u>-rohn ah-<u>kohng</u>…
– one suitcase	**– isáng maléta**	ee-<u>sahng</u> mah-<u>leh</u>-tah
– two suitcases	**– dalawáng maléta**	dah-lah-<u>wahng</u> mah-<u>leh</u>-tah
– one carry-on [piece of hand luggage]	**– isáng hand-cárry**	ee-<u>sahng</u> hahnd-<u>keh</u>-ree
How much luggage is allowed?	**Iláng bagáhe ang pinapayágan?**	ee-<u>lahng</u> bah-<u>gah</u>-heh ahng pee-nah-pah-<u>yah</u>-gahn
Which *terminal/gate*?	**Alíng *términál/gate*?**	ah-<u>leeng</u> *tehr-mee-<u>nahl</u>/gehyt*
I'd like a *window/an aisle* seat.	**Gustó ko ng upúan sa *tabí ng bintanà/gitnâ.***	goos-<u>toh</u> koh nahng oo-<u>poo</u>-ahn sah *tah-<u>bee</u> nahng been-<u>tah</u>-nah'/geet-<u>nah</u>'*
When do we *leave/arrive*?	**Anóng óras táyo *áalis/dárating*?**	ah-<u>nohng</u> <u>oh</u>-rahs <u>tah</u>-yoh *<u>ah</u>-ah-lees/dah-rah-teeng*
Is the flight delayed?	**Deláyed ba ang flight?**	dee-<u>lehyd</u> bah ahng flahyt

24

You May Hear…

Súsunod! <u>soo</u>·soo·nohd	Next!
Ang inyóng *pasapórte/tíket*, please. ahng een·<u>yohng</u> pah·sah·<u>pohr</u>·teh/ <u>tee</u>·keht plees	Your *passport/ticket*, please.
Magpapások ba kayó ng bagáhe? mahg·pah·<u>pah</u>·sohk bah kah·<u>yoh</u> nahng bah·<u>gah</u>·heh	Are you checking any luggage?
May sóbra kayóng bagáhe. mahy <u>soh</u>·brah kah·<u>yohng</u> bah·<u>gah</u>·heh	You have excess luggage.
Masyádong malakí yan na hand-cárry. mah·<u>shah</u>·dohng mah·lah·<u>kee</u> yahn nah hahnd·<u>keh</u>·ree	That's too large for a carry-on [to carry on board].
Kayó lang ang nag-impake ng bag na itó? kah·<u>yoh</u> lahng ahng nahg·eem·pah·keh nahng bahg nah ee·<u>toh</u>	Did you pack these bags yourself?
Mayroón bang nagbigáy sa inyó ng dadalhín? mahy·roh·<u>ohn</u> bahng nahg·bee·<u>gahy</u> sah een·<u>yoh</u> nahng dah·dahl·<u>heen</u>	Did anyone give you anything to carry?
Sumásakáy na… soo· <u>mah</u>·sah·<u>kahy</u> nah…	Now boarding…

Luggage

Where *is/are*…?

Saán *ang/ang mgá*…? sah·<u>ahn</u> ahng/ahng mah·<u>ngah</u>…

– the luggage carts [trolleys]

– trólleys na lalagyán ng bagáhe <u>troh</u>·lees nah lah·lahg·<u>yahn</u> nahng bah·<u>gah</u>·heh

– the luggage lockers

– lóckers ng bagáhe <u>lah</u>·kehrs nahng bah·<u>gah</u>·heh

– the baggage claim

– kuhanán ng bagáhe koo·hah·<u>nahn</u> nahng bah·<u>gah</u>·heh

25

| My luggage has been *lost/stolen*. | **Nawalâ/Nanákaw ang bagáhe ko.** nah·wah·<u>lah</u>'/nah·<u>nah</u>·kahw ahng bah·<u>gah</u>·heh koh |
| My suitcase is damaged. | **Nasirà ang maléta ko.** nah·<u>see</u>·rah' ahng mah·<u>leh</u>·tah koh |

You May Hear...

Méron ba kayóng tíket ng bagáhe? meh·rohn bah kah·<u>yohng</u> <u>tee</u>·keht nahng bah·<u>gah</u>·heh	Do you have the luggage [baggage] ticket?
Anó bang itsúra ng bagáhe ninyó? ah·<u>noh</u> bahng eet·<u>soo</u>·rah nahng bah·<u>gah</u>·heh neen·<u>yoh</u>	What does your luggage look like?
Ang inyóng bagáhe ay ipinadalá sa... ahng een·<u>yohng</u> bah·<u>gah</u>·heh ahy ee·pee·nah·dah·<u>lah</u> sah...	Your luggage was sent to...
Ang inyóng bagáhe ay maaáring dumatíng mámayáng hápon. ahng een·<u>yohng</u> bah·<u>gah</u>·heh ahy mah·ah·<u>ah</u>·reeng doo·mah·<u>teeng</u> mah·mah·<u>yahng</u> <u>hah</u>·pohn	Your luggage may arrive later today.

Finding Your Way

Where *is/are*...?	**Saán *ang/ang mgá*...?** sah·<u>ahn</u> ahng/ahng mah·<u>ngah</u>...
– the currency exchange	**– pálitan ng péra** <u>pah</u>·lee·tahn nahng <u>peh</u>·rah
– the car rental [hire]	**– rentáhan ng sasakyán** rehn·<u>tah</u>·hahn nahng sah·sahk·<u>yahn</u>
– the exit	**– labásan** lah·<u>bah</u>·sahn
– the phones	**– ang mgá teléponó** ahng mah·<u>ngah</u> teh·<u>leh</u>·poh·<u>noh</u>

How do I get to the...Hotel?	**Paáno ba akó makákapuntá sa...Hotél?** pah·ah·noh bah ah·koh mah·kah·kah·poon·tah sah...hoh·tehl
Is there...into town?	**Méron bang...na papuntá sa báyan?** meh·rohn bahng...nah pah·poon·tah sah bah·yahn
– a bus	**– bus** boos
– a train	**– tren** trehn
– a jeepney	**– dyip** dyeep

▶ For jeepney information, see page 31.

▶ For directions, see page 36.

Train

Questions

Where's the...station?	**Saán ang estasyón ng...?** sah·ahn ahng ehs·tah·shohn nahng...?
– train [railway]	**– tren** trehn
– LRT	**– LRT** ehl·ahr·tee
– MRT	**– MRT** ehm·ahr·tee
How far is it?	**Gaáno itó kalayò?** gah·ah·noh ee·toh kah·lah·yoh'
Where is the ticket counter?	**Saán ang tíket counter?** sah·ahn ahng tee·keht kahwn·tehr

▶ For ticketing, see page 20.

▶ For LRT and MRT information, see page 187.

Saán papuntá? sah-<u>ahn</u> pah-poon-<u>tah</u>   Where to?

Iláng tíket? ee-<u>lahng</u> <u>tee</u>-keht   How many tickets?

Manila is the only Philippine city with a mass transit network of trains. Trains are modern, easy to use and can save you a lot of time in your commute around the metropolis. Unfortunately, the three railways, LRT-1, LRT-2, and MRT-3, all have their own ticketing systems and they don't offer maps. The good thing, however, is that the cost per ride is inexpensive.

▶For train websites, see page 187.

Departures

Is this the train to...?   **Itó ba ang tren papuntá sa...?** ee-<u>toh</u> bah ahng trehn pah-poon-<u>tah</u> sah...

Where do I change for...?   **Saán akó magpápalít ng...?** sah-<u>ahn</u> ah-<u>koh</u> mahg-<u>pah</u>-pah-<u>leet</u> nahng...

You May Hear…

Huwág pong… hoo·<u>wahg</u> pohng…

Please do not...

– lumampás sa diláw na línya
loo·mahm·<u>pahs</u> sah dee·<u>lahw</u> nah <u>leen</u>·yah

– step past the yellow line

– pigílan ang pintô sa pagsará pee·<u>gee</u>·lahn
ahng peen·<u>toh</u>' sah pahg·sah·<u>rah</u>

– stop the doors from closing

– itupî o punítin ang inyóng mgá tíket
ee·too·<u>pee</u>' oh poo·<u>nee</u>·teen ahng een·<u>yohng</u>
mah·<u>ngah</u> <u>tee</u>·keht

– fold or destroy your tickets

Ang súsunod na tren ay deláyed.
ahng <u>soo</u>·soo·nohd nah trehn ahy dee·<u>lehyd</u>

The next train is delayed.

Kinákailángan kayóng lumípat sa Cubao.
kee·<u>nah</u>·kah·ee·<u>lah</u>·ngahn kah·<u>yohng</u>
loo·<u>mee</u>·paht sah koo·<u>bahw</u>

You have to change at Cubao.

Ang súsunod na hintô ay Cubao. ahng
<u>soo</u>·soo·nohd <u>nah</u> heen·<u>toh</u>' ahy koo·<u>bahw</u>

Next stop, Cubao.

Bus

Where's the bus station?	**Saán ang estasyón ng bus?** sah·<u>ahn</u> ahng ehs·tah·<u>shohn</u> nahng boos
How far is it?	**Gaáno kalayò itó?** gah·<u>ah</u>·noh kah·<u>lah</u>·yoh' ee·<u>toh</u>
How do I get to…?	**Papaáno akó makákapuntá sa…?** pah·pah·<u>ah</u>·noh ah·<u>koh</u> mah·<u>kah</u>·kah·poon·<u>tah</u> sah…
Is this the bus to…?	**Itó ba ang bus papuntáng…?** ee·<u>toh</u> bah ahng boos pah·poon·<u>tahng</u>…
Can you tell me when to get off?	**Pwéde ba ninyóng sabíhin sa ákin kung saán bababâ?** <u>pweh</u>·deh bah neen·<u>yohng</u> sah·<u>bee</u>·heen sah <u>ah</u>·keen koong sah·<u>ahn</u> bah·bah·<u>bah</u>'

Do I have to change buses?	**Kailángan ko bang lumípat ng bus?** kah·ee·<u>lah</u>·ngahn koh bahng loo·mee·paht nahng boos
How many stops to…?	**Iláng estasyón ba ang hiníhintuán papuntá sa…?** ee·<u>lahng</u> ehs·tah·<u>shohn</u> bah ahng hee·<u>nee</u>·heen·too·<u>ahn</u> pah·poon·tah sah…
Stop here, please!	**Pára pô!** <u>pah</u>·rah <u>poh</u>'

▶For ticketing, see page 20.

There is no municipal bus system in Metro Manila, but there are plenty of privately owned buses offering innumerable routes and running 24 hours a day. It is not easy to figure out how they work and where they're going, and there are no route maps on offer. Basically, buses follow main thoroughfares throughout the metropolis. Destinations are posted on the front window. There are few scheduled stops. Buses just pull over when a pedestrian flags them down or a passenger wants to get off. There are air-conditioned and non-air-conditioned buses. Your fare is paid to a conductor, who will issue you a paper ticket.

You May See…

HINTÚAN NG BUS	bus stop
PAKITAGÒ ANG INYÓNG TÍKET PÁRA SA INSPEKSYÓN.	Please keep your ticket for inspection.
PINDUTÍN ANG BUTÓN PÁRA HUMINTÔ ANG BUS.	Press the button to stop the bus.
EKSÁKTONG PAMASÁHE LANG PÔ.	Please give exact fare.

Other Modes of Transportation

Where's the *jeepney/tricycle* station?	**Saán ang estasyón ng *dyip/tráysikél*?** sah·<u>ahn</u> ahng ehs·tah·<u>shohn</u> nahng *dyeep/<u>trahy</u>·see·<u>kehl</u>*
Do I have to transfer [change]?	**Kailángan ko bang lumípat?** kah·ee·<u>lah</u>·ngahn koh bahng loo·<u>mee</u>·paht
Is this the *jeepney/tricycle* to…?	**Itó ba ang *dyip/tráysikél* papuntáng…?** ee·<u>toh</u> bah ahng *dyeep/<u>trahy</u>·see·<u>kehl</u>* pah·poon·<u>tahng</u>…
Is this my stop?	**Díto na ba akó bababâ?** <u>dee</u>·toh nah bah ah·<u>koh</u> bah·bah·<u>bah</u>'
Where are we?	**Saán na táyo?** sah·<u>ahn</u> nah <u>tah</u>·yoh

i

The colorful and ubiquitous **dyip** (jeepney) goes everywhere the buses don't. They're hot, cramped and their routes will make little sense to the newcomer. But you can't truly say you've been to the Philippines until you've ridden in a jeepney. Plus, fares are dirt cheap.

An alternative to the jeepney is the FX taxi. These boxy vehicles are a little more expensive, but the air conditioning makes them more bearable. For shorter routes off the main roads, you can ride a **tráysikél** (known as a tricycle in English, but it's really a motorcycle with an attached sidecar) or a **pedicab** (a bicycle with an attached sidecar). For a trip back to the old days, try a **calesa** (horse-drawn carriage).

Boat and Ferry

When is the ferry to…?	**Kailán ang férry na papuntáng…?** kah·ee·<u>lahn</u> ahng <u>feh</u>·ree nah pah·poon·<u>tahng</u>…
Where are the life jackets?	**Saán ang life jáckets?** sah·<u>ahn</u> ahng lahyf <u>jah</u>·kehts

▶For ticketing, see page 20.

LIFE BOAT	life boat
LIFE JÁCKET	life jacket

Passenger ships and ferry services are common forms of transportation in the Philippine archipelago. Standards range from huge, modern ships offering private rooms and dining, down to rickety wooden vessels that have seen better days.

The big passenger ships sailing to and from Manila travel south to all the major port cities, and offer spectacular, up-close views of the country. In the provinces, there are many offerings for local ferry service between islands. **Fast Supercats** are becoming popular, as is the **Roll On-Roll Off** service for those with vehicles. Standards vary widely at many provincial ports, so ask to see the boat first before paying.

Bicycle and Motorcycle

I'd like to rent [hire]...	**Gustó kong magrénta...** goos·<u>toh</u> kohng mahg·<u>rehn</u>·tah...
– a bicycle	**– ng bisikléta** nahng bee·seek·<u>leh</u>·tah
– a mountain bike	**– ng mountain bike** nahng <u>mahwn</u>·tehn bahyk
– a motorcycle	**– ng motorsíklo** nahng moh·tohr·<u>seek</u>·loh
How much per day/week?	**Magkáno báwat *araw/linggó*?** mahg·<u>kah</u>·noh <u>bah</u>·waht <u>ah</u>·rahw/leeng·<u>goh</u>
Can I have a helmet/lock?	**Pwéde bang humirám ng *hélmet/ kandádo*?** pweh·deh bahng hoo·mee·<u>rahm</u> nahng <u>hel</u>·meht/kahn·<u>dah</u>·doh

Taxi

Where can I get a taxi?	**Saán pwédeng kumúha ng táksi?** sah·ahn pweh·dehng koo·moo·hah nahng tahk·see
Do you have the number for a taxi?	**Méron ba kayóng teléponó ng táksi?** meh·rohn bah kah·yohng teh·leh·poh·noh nahng tahk·see
I'd like a taxi…	**Gustó ko ng táksi…** goos·toh koh nahng tahk·see…
– now	**– ngayón din** ngah·yohn deen
– in an hour	**– sa loób ng isáng óras** sah loh·ohb nahng ee·sahng oh·rahs
– for tomorrow at…	**– búkas ng alás…** boo·kahs nahng ah·lahs…
Pick me up at…	**Daánan ninyó akó sa…** dah·ah·nahn neen·yoh ah·koh sah…
I'm going to…	**Púpuntá akó sa…** poo·poon·tah ah·koh sah…
– this address	**– adrés na itó** ah·drehs nah ee·toh
– the *international/ domestic* airport	**– *internásyonal/doméstik* airport** een·tehr·nah·shoh·nahl/doh·mehs·teek ehyr·pohrt
– the *LRT/MRT* station	**– estasyón ng *LRT/MRT*** ehs·tah·shohn nahng ehl·ahr·tee/ehm·ahr·tee
I'm late.	**Late na akó.** lehyt nah ah·koh
Can you drive *faster/slower*?	**Pwéde ba ninyóng *bilisán/bagálan* ang pag-dríve?** pweh·deh bah neen·yohng bee·lee·sahn/bah·gah·lahn ahng pahg·drahyv
Can you take a direct route?	**Pwéde ba kayóng dumaán sa dirétsong rúta?** pweh·deh bah kah·yohng doo·mah·ahn sah dee·reht·sohng roo·tah

How much?	**Magkáno?** mahg·<u>kah</u>·noh
You said it would cost…	**Sábi ninyó áabútin lang itó ng…** <u>sah</u>·bee neen·<u>yoh</u> ah·ah·<u>boo</u>·teen lahng ee·<u>toh</u> nahng…
Keep the change.	**Sa inyó na ang suklî.** sah een·<u>yoh</u> nah ahng sook·<u>lee</u>'

You May Hear…

Saán kayó papuntá?
sah·<u>ahn</u> kah·<u>yoh</u> pah·poon·<u>tah</u>

Where to?

Anó ang adrés? ah·<u>noh</u> ahng ahd·<u>rehs</u>

What's the address?

Sóri pô péro hindî ko kayó pwédeng ihatíd doón. <u>soh</u>·ree poh' <u>peh</u>·roh heen·<u>dee</u>' koh kah·<u>yoh</u> <u>pweh</u>·dehng ee·hah·<u>teed</u> doh·<u>ohn</u>

Sorry, but I can't take you there.

i

Many tourists find that one of the great pleasures of traveling in the Philippines is the inexpensive and widely available taxi service. Some taxi drivers will ask for a fixed rate. Unless you feel the price is fine, insist on going by the meter. If the driver doesn't want to turn on the meter, wait for another cab.

Taxis from the airports do not use the meter. Instead, passengers must pay fixed rates, which are rather high by local standards. A common trick to avoid the fixed fare at airports is to walk one floor up to the departure area, and catch a cab that has just dropped off a passenger.

Car

Car Rental [Hire]

Where's the car rental [hire]?	**Saán ang rentáhan ng sasakyán?** sah·<u>ahn</u> ahng rehn·<u>tah</u>·hahn nahng sah·sahk·<u>yahn</u>

I'd like…	**Gustó ko…** goos·<u>toh</u> koh…
– an automatic/ a manual	– **ng *automátic/ng mánual*** nahng oh·toh·<u>mah</u>·teek/nahng <u>mahn</u>·wahl
– a 2-/4-door	– **ng *twó-/four-door*** nahng <u>too</u>/<u>fohwr</u> door
– air conditioning	– **ng may aírcon** nahng mahy <u>ehyr</u>·kohn
– a car seat	– **ng may car seat** nahng mahy cahr seet
How much…?	**Magkáno…?** mahg·<u>kah</u>·noh…
– per *day/week*	– **báwat *áraw/linggó*** <u>bah</u>·waht <u>ah</u>·rahw/ leeng·<u>goh</u>
– for…days	– **pára sa…na áraw** <u>pah</u>·rah sah…nah <u>ah</u>·rahw
– per kilometer	– **báwat kilométro** <u>bah</u>·waht kee·loh·<u>meh</u>·troh
Are there any discounts?	**Méron bang diskwénto?** <u>meh</u>·rohn bahng dees·<u>kwehn</u>·toh

You May Hear…

Ang pasapórte ninyó, please. ahng pah·sah·<u>pohr</u>·teh neen·<u>yoh</u> plees	Your passport, please.
Kailángan ko ng depósito. kah·ee·<u>lah</u>·ngahn koh nahng deh·<u>poh</u>·see·toh	I'll need a deposit.
***Inisyalán/Pirmahán* díto.** ee·nees·yah·<u>lan</u>/peer·mah·<u>hahn</u> <u>dee</u>·toh	*Initial/Sign* here.

In the big cities especially, car rental agencies abound. Prices are generally quite reasonable and you'll find all the latest models. You will need a foreign driver's license in English, or an international driver's license. A great way to get around is to rent a car with a driver. Driving in the Philippines can be unnerving for the first-timer, so a chauffeur can do all the work, while you sit back and enjoy the sights.

Gas [Petrol] Station

Where's the gas [petrol] station?	**Saán ang gásolinahán?** sah·ahn ahng gah·soh·lee·nah·hahn
Fill it up, please.	**Full tank, please.** fool tahnk plees
…pesos, please.	**…píso, please.** …pee·soh plees
I'll pay in cash/by credit card.	**Magbabáyad akó ng** cash/crédit card. mahg·bah·bah·yahd ah·koh nahng kahsh/kreh·deet kahrd

You May See…

UNLEÁDED	unleaded
RÉGULAR	regular
SÚPER	super
BÍOFÚEL	biofuel
PRÉMIUM	premium
DÍESEL	diesel
SELF-SÉRVICE	self-service
FULL-SÉRVICE	full-service

Asking Directions

Is this the way to…?	**Itó ba ang daán papuntáng…?** ee·toh bah ahng dah·ahn pah·poon·tahng…
How far is it to…?	**Gaáno itó kalayò sa…?** gah·ah·noh ee·toh kah·lah·yoh' sah…
Where's…?	**Saán…?** sah·ahn…
– …Street	**– ang…Stréet** ahng…ees·treet
– this address	**– ang adrés na itó** ahng ahd·rehs nah ee·toh
– the highway [motorway]	**– ang híghway** ahng hahy·wehy

Can you show me on the map?	**Pwéde ba ninyóng iturò sa mápa?** <u>pweh</u>·deh bah neen·<u>yohng</u> ee·<u>too</u>·roh' sah <u>mah</u>·pah
I'm lost.	**Nawáwalâ akó.** nah·<u>wah</u>·wah·<u>lah</u>' ah·<u>koh</u>

You May Hear...

kaliwâ/kánan kah·lee·<u>wah</u>'/<u>kah</u>·nahn	left/right
sa/sa may **kánto** _sah/sah mahy_ <u>kahn</u>·toh	_on/around_ the corner
kabilâ kah·bee·<u>lah</u>'	opposite
sa likód sah lee·<u>kohd</u>	behind
sunód sa soo·<u>nohd</u> sah	next to
paglampás pahg·lahm·<u>pahs</u>	after
bágo <u>bah</u>·goh	before
north/south nohrt/sohwt	north/south
east/west eest/wehst	east/west
sa may tráffic light sah mahy <u>trah</u>·feek lahyt	at the traffic light
sa may ínterséksyon sah mahy een·tehr·<u>sehk</u>·shohn	at the intersection

You May See...

MANATÍLI SA KALIWÂ	keep left
MANATÍLI SA KÁNAN	keep right
BÁWAL PUMÁSOK	no entry
BÁWAL PUMARÁDA	no parking
BÁWAL MAG-Ú-TURN	no U-turn
HINTÔ	stop
MAGBIGÁY-DAÁN	yield

Parking

Can I park here?	**Pwéde bang pumaráda díto?** <u>pweh</u>·deh bahng poo·mah·<u>rah</u>·dah <u>dee</u>·toh
How much…?	**Magkáno…?** mahg·<u>kah</u>·noh…
– per hour	**– ang báwat óras** ahng <u>bah</u>·waht <u>oh</u>·rahs
– per day	**– ang báwat áraw** ahng <u>bah</u>·waht <u>ah</u>·rahw
– overnight	**– ang magdamág** ahng mahg·dah·<u>mahg</u>

For a city as crowded as Manila, finding a parking spot for your car is surprisingly not much of a problem. That's because almost everywhere you go, you'll come across someone whose job it is to watch over a few parking spots on that particular street. These guys are not "official" in any way, but they can generally be relied upon to watch your car, even for several days. Just remember to tip them when you leave.

More organized parking lots and garages are readily available at the many malls and around the business districts. Rates are charged by the hour and the prices are extremely reasonable.

Breakdown and Repairs

My car *broke down/won't start*.	***Nasirà/Áyaw mag-stárt* ang kótse ko.** nah·<u>see</u>·rah'/<u>ah</u>·yahw <u>mahg</u>·ees·<u>tahrt</u> ahng <u>koht</u>·seh koh
Can you fix it (today)?	**Káya ba ninyóng ayúsin (ngayóng áraw na itó)?** <u>kah</u>·yah bah neen·<u>yohng</u> ah·<u>yoo</u>·seen (ngah·<u>yohng</u> <u>ah</u>·rahw nah ee·<u>toh</u>)
When will it be ready?	**Kailán matatápos?** kah·ee·<u>lahn</u> mah·tah·<u>tah</u>·pohs
How much?	**Magkáno?** mahg·<u>kah</u>·noh

If you are renting a vehicle and you require roadside assistance, your best first option is to call the rental agency where you hired the car. If you cannot get through to the car rental agency, dial 117 for emergency police assistance.

Accidents

There was an accident.	**Mérong aksidénte.** <u>meh</u>·rohng ahk·see·<u>dehn</u>·teh
Call *an ambulance/the police.*	**Tumáwag *ng ambulánsya/ng pulís.*** too·<u>mah</u>·wahg *nahng ahm·boo·<u>lahn</u>·shah/ nahng poo·<u>lees</u>*

Accommodations

Essential

Can you recommend a hotel?	**Pwéde ba kayóng magrékomendá ng hotél?** <u>pweh</u>·deh bah kah·<u>yohng</u> mahg·<u>reh</u>·koh·mehn·<u>dah</u> nahng hoh·<u>tehl</u>
I have a reservation.	**Méron akóng resérbasyón.** <u>meh</u>·rohn ah·<u>kohng</u> reh·<u>sehr</u>·bah·<u>shohn</u>
My name is…	**…ang pangálan ko.** …ahng pah·<u>ngah</u>·lahn koh
Do you have a room…?	**Méron ba kayóng kuwárto…?** <u>meh</u>·rohn bah kah·<u>yohng</u> koo·<u>wahr</u>·toh…
– for *one/two*	– **pára sa *isá/dalawá*** <u>pah</u>·rah sah *ee·<u>sah</u>/ dah·lah·<u>wah</u>*
– with a bathroom	– **na may bányo** nah mahy <u>bahn</u>·yoh
– with air conditioning	– **na may aírcon** nah mahy <u>ehyr</u>·kohn

For...	**Pára...** pah·rah...
– tonight	**– sa ngayóng gabí** sah ngah·<u>yohng</u> gah·<u>bee</u>
– two nights	**– sa dalawáng gabí** sah dah·lah·<u>wahng</u> gah·<u>bee</u>
– one week	**– sa isáng linggó** sah ee·<u>sahng</u> leeng·<u>goh</u>
How much?	**Magkáno?** mahg·<u>kah</u>·noh
Is there anything cheaper?	**Méron bang mas múra?** <u>meh</u>·rohn bahng mahs <u>moo</u>·rah
Can I see the room?	**Pwéde ko bang makíta ang kuwárto?** <u>pweh</u>·deh koh bahng mah·<u>kee</u>·tah ahng koo·<u>wahr</u>·toh
I'll take it.	**Kukúnin ko itó.** koo·<u>koo</u>·neen koh ee·<u>toh</u>
When's check-out?	**Kailán ang check-out?** kah·ee·<u>lahn</u> ahng chehk-ahwt
Can I leave this in the safe?	**Pwéde bang iwánan itó sa vault?** <u>pweh</u>·deh bahng ee·<u>wah</u>·nahn ee·<u>toh</u> sah vohlt
Can I leave my bags?	**Pwéde bang iwánan ang áking mgá bag?** <u>pweh</u>·deh bahng ee·<u>wah</u>·nahn ahng <u>ah</u>·keeng mah·<u>ngah</u> bahg
Can I have my *bill/ receipt*?	**Pwéde bang kúnin ang áking *bill/ resíbo*?** <u>pweh</u>·deh bahng <u>koo</u>·neen ahng <u>ah</u>·keeng *beel/reh·<u>see</u>·boh*
I'll pay *in cash/by credit card*.	**Magbabáyad akó ng *cash/crédit card*.** mahg·bah·<u>bah</u>·yahd ah·<u>koh</u> nahng *kahsh/<u>kreh</u>·deet kahrd*

i If you show up in the Philippines without a hotel reservation, there are a variety of resources available to you. The Ninoy Aquino International Airport (NAIA) in Manila and the Mactan International Airport in Cebu have representatives from various hotels waiting as you leave Customs. You might also find brochure racks outside of Customs advertising different hotels. If you have a general idea of the area of town you want to stay in, ask a taxi driver to take you there. With a little hunting, you're likely to find a suitable hotel room in no time. You can also contact the Department of Tourism for recommendations on places to stay; contact information can be found online.

▶ For useful websites, see page 187.

Finding Lodging

Can you recommend…?	**Pwéde ba kayóng magrékomendá…?** pweh·deh bah kah·yohng mahg·reh·koh·mehn·dah…
– a hotel	**– ng hotél** nahng hoh·tehl
– a hostel	**– ng hóstel** nahng hohs·tehl
– a beach resort	**– ng beach resórt** nahng beech reh·sohrt
– a bed and breakfast	**– ng bed and bréakfast** nahng behd ehnd brehk·fahst
What is it near?	**Anó ang malápit díto?** ah·noh ahng mah·lah·peet dee·toh
How do I get there?	**Paáno akó makákapuntá doón?** pah·ah·noh ah·koh mah·kah·kah·poon·tah doh·ohn

You May Hear…

Mérong hotél sa báyan na may bakánte pang kuwárto.
meh·rohng hoh·tehl sah bah·yahn nah mahy bah·kahn·teh pahng koo·wahr·toh

There's a hotel downtown with a room available.

Ireresérba ko ba iyón?
ee·reh·reh·sehr·bah koh bah ee·yohn

Should I book it?

Kailángan ko ang iyóng crédit card.
kah·ee·lah·ngahn koh ahng ee·yohng kreh·deet kahrd

I'll need your credit card.

Inaasáhan ka nilá búkas.
ee·nah·ah·sah·hahn kah nee·lah boo·kahs

They're expecting you tomorrow.

---

i Travelers in the Philippines will find a complete range of accommodations available, from international 5-star hotel chains, to 3- and 4-star business hotels and all the way down to budget hotels and guesthouses. No matter where you stay, it helps to have a reservation, but especially so at guesthouses, as they have fewer rooms and fill up quickly.

At the Hotel

I have a reservation.	**Méron akóng resérbasyón.** <u>meh</u>·rohn ah·<u>kohng</u> reh·<u>sehr</u>·bah·<u>shohn</u>
My name is…	**…ang pangálan ko.** …ahng pah·<u>ngah</u>·lahn <u>koh</u>
Do you have a room…?	**Méron ba kayóng kuwárto…?** <u>meh</u>·rohn bah kah·<u>yohng</u> koo·<u>wahr</u>·toh…
– for *one/two*	**– pára sa *isá/dalawá*** <u>pah</u>·rah sah *ee·<u>sah</u>/ dah·lah·<u>wah</u>*
– with a *bathroom [toilet]/shower*	**– na may *bányo/shówer*** nah mahy *<u>bahn</u>·yoh/<u>shah</u>·wehr*
– with air conditioning	**– na may aircon** nah mahy <u>ehyr</u>·kohn
– that's handicapped [disabled] accessible	**– na madalíng puntahán ng may kapansánan** nah mah·dah·<u>leeng</u> poon·tah·<u>han</u> nahng mahy kah·pahn·<u>sah</u>·nahn
– that's *smoking/ non-smoking*	**– na *smóking/non-smóking*** nah *ees·<u>mohw</u>·keeng/nahn·ees·<u>mohw</u>·keeng*
For…	**Pára…** <u>pah</u>·rah…
– tonight	**– sa ngayóng gabí** sah ngah·<u>yohng</u> gah·bee
– two nights	**– sa dalawáng gabí** sah dah·lah·<u>wahng</u> gah·bee
– a week	**– sa isáng linggó** sah ee·<u>sahng</u> leeng·goh

▶ For numbers, see page 181.

Do you have…?	**Méron ba kayóng…?** <u>meh</u>·rohn bah kah·<u>yohng</u>…
– a computer	**– kompyúter** kohmp·<u>yoo</u>·tehr
– an elevator [a lift]	**– élevator** <u>eh</u>·leh·vehy·tohr
– a fax	**– fax** fahx
– (wireless) internet service	**– (wíreless) ínternet sérvice** (<u>wahyr</u>·lehs) <u>een</u>·tehr·neht <u>sehr</u>·vees

Do you have...?	**Méron ba kayóng...?** <u>meh</u>·rohn bah kah·<u>yohng</u>...
– housekeeping services	– **tagalínis** tah·gah·<u>lee</u>·nees
– laundry service	– **tagalabá** tah·gah·lah·<u>bah</u>
– room service	– **room sérvice** room <u>sehr</u>·vees
– a pool	– **pool** pool
– a gym	– **gym** jeem
I need...	**Kailángan ko...** kah·ee·<u>lah</u>·ngahn koh...
– an extra bed	– **ng ékstra na káma** nahng <u>ehks</u>·trah nah <u>kah</u>·mah
– a cot	– **ng tihéras** nahng tee·<u>heh</u>·rahs
– a crib	– **ng krib** nahng kreeb

You May Hear...

Ang *pasapórte/crédit card* nilá, please. ahng *pah·sah·<u>pohr</u>·teh/<u>kreh</u>·deet kahrd* nee·<u>lah</u> plees	Your *passport/credit card*, please.
Sagután ang form na itó. sah·goo·<u>tahn</u> ahng fohrm nah ee·<u>toh</u>	Fill out this form.
Pumírma díto. poo·<u>meer</u>·mah <u>dee</u>·toh	Sign here.

Price

How much per *night/week*?	**Magkáno báwat *gabí/linggó*?** mahg·<u>kah</u>·noh bah·waht *gah·<u>bee</u>/leeng·<u>goh</u>*
Does that include sales tax [VAT]?	**Kasáma ba ríto ang VAT?** kah·<u>sah</u>·mah bah <u>ree</u>·toh ahng vaht
Are there any discounts?	**Méron bang diskwénto?** <u>meh</u>·rohn bahng dees·<u>kwehn</u>·toh

Decisions

Can I see the room?	**Pwéde ko bang makíta ang kuwárto?** pweh·deh koh bahng mah·kee·tah ahng koo·wahr·toh
I'd like…room.	**Gustó ko ng…kuwárto.** goos·toh koh nahng…koo·wahr·toh
– a better	**– mas maáyos na** mahs mah·ah·yohs nah
– a bigger	**– mas malakí na** mahs mah·lah·kee nah
– a cheaper	**– mas múra na** mahs moo·rah nah
– a quieter	**– mas tahímik na** mahs tah·hee·meek nah
I'll take it.	**Kukúnin ko itó.** koo·koo·neen koh ee·toh
No, I won't take it.	**Hindî ko kukúnin itó.** heen·dee'koh koo·koo·neen ee·toh

Questions

Where's…?	**Saán…?** sah·ahn…
– the bar	**– ang bar** ahng bahr
– the bathroom [toilet]	**– ang bányo** ahng bahn·yoh
– the elevator [lift]	**– ang élevator** ahng eh·leh·vehy·tohr
– the pool	**– ang pool** ahng pool
Can I have…?	**Pwéde bang humingî ng…?** pweh·deh bahng hoo·mee·ngee' nahng…
– a blanket	**– kúmot** koo·moht
– an iron	**– plántsa** plahn·tsah
– the room key/ key card	**– susì ng kuwárto/key card** soo·see' nahng koo·wahr·toh/kee kahrd
– a pillow	**– únan** oo·nahn
– soap	**– sabón** sah·bohn
– toilet paper	**– tísyu** tees·yoo
– a towel	**– tuwálya** too·wahl·yah

Do you have an adapter for this?	**Méron ba kayóng adápter pára díto?** meh·rohn bah kah·yohng ah·dahp·tehr pah·rah dee·toh
How do I turn on the lights?	**Paáno ko bubuksán ang ílaw?** pah·ah·noh koh boo·book·sahn ahng ee·lahw
Can you wake me at…?	**Pwéde ba ninyó akóng gisíngin ng alás…?** pweh·deh bah neen·yoh ah·kohng gee·see·ngeen nahng ah·lahs…
Can I leave this in the safe?	**Pwéde ko bang iwánan itó sa vault?** pweh·deh koh bahng ee·wah·nahn ee·toh sah vohlt
Can I have my things from the safe?	**Pwéde ko bang kúnin ang mgá gámit ko sa vault?** pweh·deh koh bahng koo·neen ahng mah·ngah gah·meet koh sah vohlt
Is there *mail [post]/ a message* for me?	**Méron ba akóng *súlat/mensáhe*?** meh·rohn bah ah·kohng soo·laht/ mehn·sah·heh

You May See…

TÚLAK/HÁTAK	push/pull
BÁNYO/CR	bathroom/restroom [toilet]
SHÓWER	shower
ÉLEVATOR	elevator [lift]
LAUNDRY	laundry
HUWÁG ISTÓRBUHIN	do not disturb
FIRE ÉXIT	fire door
WÁKE-UP CALL	wake-up call

Problems

There's a problem.	**Mérong probléma.** <u>meh</u>·rohng prohb·<u>leh</u>·mah
I lost my *key/key card*.	**Nawalâ ko ang áking *susì/key card*.** nah·wah·<u>lah</u>' koh ahng <u>ah</u>·keeng *<u>soo</u>·see'/kee kahrd*
I'm locked out of the room.	**Nasaradúhan akó.** nah·sah·rah·<u>doo</u>·hahn ah·<u>koh</u>
There's no *hot water/toilet paper*.	**Waláng *maínit na túbig/tísyu*.** wah·<u>lahng</u> mah·<u>ee</u>·neet nah <u>too</u>·beeg/<u>tees</u>·yoo
The room is dirty.	**Madumí ang kuwárto.** mah·doo·<u>mee</u> ahng koo·<u>wahr</u>·toh
There are bugs in the room.	**Mérong súrot sa kuwárto.** <u>meh</u>·rohng <u>soo</u>·roht sah koo·<u>wahr</u>·toh
…doesn't work.	**…ay hindî gumagána.** …ahy heen·<u>dee</u>' goo·mah·<u>gah</u>·nah
Can you fix…?	**Pwéde ba ninyóng ayúsin…?** <u>pweh</u>·deh neen·<u>yohng</u> ah·<u>yoo</u>·seen…
– the air conditioning	**– ang aírcon** ahng <u>ehyr</u>·kohn
– the fan	**– ang béntiladór** ahng <u>behn</u>·tee·lah·<u>dohr</u>
– the heater	**– ang héater** ahng <u>hee</u>·tehr
– the light	**– ang ílaw** ahng <u>ee</u>·lahw
– the TV	**– ang TV** ahng <u>tee</u>·vee
– the toilet	**– ang inidóro** ahng ee·nee·<u>doh</u>·roh
I'd like another room.	**Gustó ko ng ibáng kuwárto.** goos·<u>toh</u> koh nahng ee·<u>bahng</u> koo·<u>wahr</u>·toh

The standard voltage used in the Philippines is 220 volts, 60 Hz. Also quite common are 110-volt outlets, which can be found in many hotel rooms alongside the 220-volt outlets. Most plugs are of the flat, two-pin type, so you may need an adapter to plug in your electronic items. To avoid hassles, especially in the provinces, it is best to bring your own universal adapter.

Check-out

When's check-out?	**Kailán ang check-out?** kah·ee·*lahn* ahng chehk·ahwt
Can I leave my bags here until…?	**Pwéde bang iwánan ang áking mgá bag hanggáng…?** *pweh*·deh bahng ee·*wah*·nahn ahng *ah*·keeng mah·*ngah* bahg hahng·*gahng*…

▶ For time, see page 183.

Can I have *an itemized bill/a receipt*?	**Pwéde bang makakúha *ng nakadetályeng bill/resíbo*?** *pweh*·deh bahng mah·kah·*koo*·hah nahng *nah·kah·deh·tahl·yehng* beel/reh·*see*·boh
I'll pay *in cash/by credit card*.	**Magbabáyad akó *ng cash/crédit card*.** mahg·bah·*bah*·yahd ah·*koh* nahng kahsh/*kreh*·deet kahrd

You May Hear…

Lahát ng nakúha ninyó ay…
lah·*haht* nahng nah·*koo*·hah neen·*yoh* ahy…

Your total is…

Paáno ninyó gustó itóng bayáran?
pah·*ah*·noh neen·*yoh* goos·*toh* ee·*tohng* bah·*yah*·rahn

How would you like to pay?

Tipping is very common in the Philippines and will be greatly appreciated by those who are providing you with service. There is no required amount, as the tip will often depend on the level of service and your level of satisfaction. However, for small services rendered by housekeeping, room service, a doorman or a bartender, you can never go wrong handing over a few pesos. If these people have been looking after you for several days, the tip will be larger.

Renting

I reserved...	**Nagparesérba akó...** nahg·pah·reh·<u>sehr</u>·bah ah·<u>koh</u>...
– an apartment	**– ng apártment** nahng ah·<u>pahrt</u>·mehnt
– a cabin	**– ng kábin** nahng <u>kah</u>·been
– a condo	**– ng kóndo** nahng <u>kohn</u>·doh
– a room	**– ng kuwárto** nahng koo·<u>wahr</u>·toh
My name is...	**...ang pangálan ko.** ...ahng pah·<u>ngah</u>·lahn koh
Can I have the *key/key card*?	**Pwéde ko bang kúnin ang *susi/key card*?** <u>pweh</u>·deh koh bahng <u>koo</u>·neen ahng *<u>soo</u>·see'/ kee kahrd*
Are there...?	**Méron bang...?** <u>meh</u>·rohn bahng...
– dishes	**– mgá pinggán** mah·<u>ngah</u> peeng·<u>gahn</u>
– pillows	**– mgá únan** mah·<u>ngah</u> <u>oo</u>·nahn
– sheets	**– bed sheets** behd sheets
– towels	**– mgá tuwálya** mah·<u>ngah</u> too·<u>wahl</u>·yah
– utensils	**– mgá gámit sa pagkáin** mah·<u>ngah</u> <u>gah</u>·meet sah pahg·<u>kah</u>·een

When do I put out the *trash [rubbish]/recycling*?	**Kailán ko ilalabás ang *basúra/mgá pwédeng i-recýcle*?** kah·ee·<u>lahn</u> koh ee·lah·lah·<u>bahs</u> ahng *bah·<u>soo</u>·rah/mah·<u>ngah</u> pweh·dehng ee·reh·<u>sahy</u>·kehl*
How does the...work?	**Paáno ba ginagámit ang...?** pah·<u>ah</u>·noh bah gee·nah·<u>gah</u>·meet ahng...
The...is broken.	**Ang...ay sirâ.** ahng...ahy see·<u>rah</u>'
– air conditioner	**– aírcon** <u>ehyr</u>·kohn
– dishwasher	**– díshwasher** <u>deesh</u>·wah·shehr
– freezer	**– fréezer** <u>free</u>·zehr
– heater	**– héater** <u>hee</u>·tehr
– microwave	**– mícrowáve** <u>mahyk</u>·roh·<u>wehyv</u>
– refrigerator	**– réfrigerátor** <u>rehf</u>·ree·jeh·<u>rehy</u>·tohr
– stove	**– kalán** kah·<u>lahn</u>
– washing machine	**– wáshing machíne** <u>wah</u>·sheeng mah·<u>sheen</u>

Household Items

I need...	**Kailángan ko ng...** kah·ee·<u>lah</u>·ngahn koh nahng...
– an adapter	**– adapter** ah·<u>dahp</u>·tehr
– aluminum [kitchen] foil	**– alúmum foil** ah·<u>loo</u>·mee·noom fohyl
– a bottle opener	**– pambukás ng bóte** pahm·boo·<u>kahs</u> nahng <u>boh</u>·teh
– a broom	**– walís** wah·<u>lees</u>
– a can opener	**– ábre láta** <u>ahb</u>·reh·<u>lah</u>·tah
– a corkscrew	**– córkscrew** <u>kohrk</u>·skroo
– garbage [rubbish] bags	**– mgá súpot ng basúra** mah·<u>ngah</u> <u>soo</u>·poht nahng bah·<u>soo</u>·rah
– a lightbulb	**– bombílya** bohm·<u>beel</u>·yah
– matches	**– mgá pósporó** mah·<u>ngah</u> <u>pohs</u>·poh·<u>roh</u>

– a mop	– **mop** mahp
– napkins	– **mgá nápkin** mah·ngah nahp·keen
– paper towels	– **páper tówels** pehy·pehr tah·wehls
– plastic wrap [cling film]	– **plástik na pambálot** plahs·teek nah pahm·bah·loht
– a plunger	– **pambómba ng inidóro** pahm·bohm·bah nahng ee·nee·doh·roh
– scissors	– **guntíng** goon·teeng
– a vacuum cleaner	– **vácuum cléaner** vahk·yoom clee·nehr

▶ For dishes and utensils, see page 73.

▶ For oven temperatures, see page 187.

Hostel

Is there a bed available?	**Méron pa bang bakánteng káma?** meh·rohn pah bahng bah·kahn·tehng kah·mah
Can I have…?	**Pwéde ba akóng magkaroón ng…?** pweh·deh bah ah·kohng mahg·kah·roh·ohn nahng…
– a *single/double* room	– **isáng/dalawáng kuwárto** ee·sahng/ dah·lah·wahng koo·wahr·toh
– a blanket	– **kúmot** koo·moht
– a pillow	– **únan** oo·nahn
– sheets	– **sheets** sheets
– a towel	– **tuwálya** too·wahl·yah
Do you have lockers?	**Méron ba kayóng lóckers?** meh·rohn bah kah·yohng lah·kehrs
When do you lock up?	**Anóng óras kayó nagsasará?** ah·nohng oh·rahs kah·yoh nahg·sah·sah·rah

| Do I need a membership card? | **Kailángan ko ba ng mémbership card?** kah-ee-<u>lah</u>-ngahn koh bah nahng <u>mehm</u>-behr-sheep kahrd |
| Here's my International Student Card. | **Éto ang áking Internátional Stúdent Card.** <u>eh</u>-toh ahng <u>ah</u>-keeng een-tehr-<u>nah</u>-shoh-nahl <u>stoo</u>-dehnt kahrd |

 Travelers on a budget will have no problem finding inexpensive accommodation in the Philippines. Traditional backpackers' hostels are not very common, but you will find a wide range of guesthouses, pensions and cottage-type rooms that are more than suitable. As one would expect with rooms in this category, the quality of the accommodation can vary widely. It helps to do your research beforehand, or to take a little time to traverse the area and see the rooms for yourself. Provincial towns, as well as mountain and beach areas, are generally the best places to find budget accommodation. Locals can point you in the right direction.

Camping

Can I camp here?	**Pwéde bang mag-kámping díto?** <u>pweh</u>-deh bahng mahg-<u>kahm</u>-peeng <u>dee</u>-toh
Where's the campsite?	**Saán ang cámpsite?** sah-<u>ahn</u> ahng <u>kahmp</u>-sahyt
Are there…?	**Méron bang…?** <u>meh</u>-rohn bahng…
– cooking facilities	**– mgá pasilidád pára sa paglulutò** mah-<u>ngah</u> pah-see-lee-<u>dahd</u> <u>pah</u>-rah sah pahg-loo-<u>loo</u>-toh'
– electric outlets	**– mgá óutlet ng koryénte** mah-<u>ngah</u> <u>ahwt</u>-leht nahng kohr-<u>yehn</u>-teh
– laundry facilities	**– mgá pasilidád sa paglalabá** mah-<u>ngah</u> pah-see-lee-<u>dahd</u> sah pahg-lah-lah-<u>bah</u>
– showers	**– mgá shówer** mah-<u>ngah</u> <u>shah</u>-wehr

| What is the charge per *day/week*? | **Magkáno ang báyad báwat *áraw/ linggó*?** mahg·<u>kah</u>·noh ahng <u>bah</u>·yahd <u>bah</u>·waht <u>ah</u>·rahw/leeng·<u>goh</u> |

You May See...

TÚBIG INÚMIN	drinking water
BÁWAL ANG MAG-KÁMPING	no camping
BÁWAL ANG *APÓY/MAG-ÍHAW*	no *fires/barbecues*

▶ For household items, see page 50.

▶ For dishes and utensils, see page 73.

Internet and Communications

Essential

Where's an internet cafe?	**Saán may ínternet café?** sah·<u>ahn</u> mahy <u>een</u>·tehr·neht kah·<u>fehy</u>
Can I *access the internet/check e-mail*?	**Pwéde bang *makagámit ng ínternet/ makapág-check ng é-maíl*?** pweh·deh bahng *mah·kah·<u>gah</u>·meet nahng <u>een</u>·tehr·<u>neht</u>/ mah·kah·<u>pahg</u>·chehk nahng <u>ee</u>·mehyl*
How much per (half) hour?	**Magkáno sa báwat (kalaháting) óras?** mahg·<u>kah</u>·noh sah <u>bah</u>·waht (kah·lah·<u>hah</u>·teeng) <u>oh</u>·rahs
How do I *connect/log on*?	**Paáno akó *makáka-connéct/maglá-log on*?** pah·<u>ah</u>·noh ah·<u>koh</u> *mah·<u>kah</u>·kah·koh·<u>nehkt</u>/ mahg·<u>lah</u>·lahg ohn*
Where's the pay phone?	**Saán ang pay phone?** sah·<u>ahn</u> ahng pehy fohn

A phone card, please.	**Isáng phone card, please.** ee-<u>sahng</u> fohn kahrd plees
Can I have your phone number?	**Pwéde ko bang makúha ang númeró ng teléponó nilá?** <u>pweh</u>-deh koh bahng mah-<u>koo</u>-hah ahng <u>noo</u>-meh-<u>roh</u> nahng teh-leh-poh-noh nee-<u>lah</u>
Here's my *number/e-mail*.	**Éto ang *númeró ng teléponó/é-mail* ko.** <u>eh</u>-toh ahng <u>noo</u>-meh-<u>roh</u> nahng teh-<u>leh</u>-poh-<u>noh</u>/ <u>ee</u>-mehyl koh
Call/E-mail me.	***Tawágan/É-mail* ninyó akó.** tah-<u>wah</u>-gahn/ <u>ee</u>-mehyl neen-<u>yoh</u> ah-<u>koh</u>
Hello. This is…	**Helló. Si…itó.** heh-<u>loh</u> see…ee-<u>toh</u>
Can I speak to…?	**Pwéde bang makaúsap si…?** <u>pweh</u>-deh bahng mah-kah-<u>oo</u>-sahp see…
Can you repeat that?	**Pwéde ba ninyóng ulítin iyón?** <u>pweh</u>-deh bah neen-<u>yohng</u> oo-<u>lee</u>-teen ee-<u>yohn</u>
I'll call back later.	**Tatawágan kitá mamayâ.** tah-tah-<u>wah</u>-gahn kee-<u>tah</u> mah-mah-<u>yah</u>'
Bye.	**Bye.** bahy
Where's the post office?	**Saán ang post óffice?** sah-<u>ahn</u> ahng pohst <u>oh</u>-fees
I'd like to send this to…	**Gustó kong ipadalá itó sa…** goos-<u>toh</u> kohng ee-pah-dah-<u>lah</u> ee-<u>toh</u> sah…

Computer, Internet and E-mail

Where's an internet cafe?	**Saán may ínternet café?** sah-<u>ahn</u> mahy <u>een</u>-tehr-neht kah-<u>fehy</u>
Does it have wireless internet?	**Méron bang wíreless ínternet?** <u>meh</u>-rohn bahng <u>wahyr</u>-lehs <u>een</u>-tehr-<u>neht</u>

How do I turn the computer *on/off*?	**Paáno ko *bubuksán/papatayín* ang kompyúter?** pah·ah·noh koh *boo·book·sahn/ pah·pah·tah·yeen* ahng kohmp·yoo·tehr
Can I…?	**Pwéde bang…?** pweh·deh bahng…
– access the internet	**– makagámit ng ínternet** mah·kah·gah·meet nahng een·tehr·neht
– check e-mail	**– makapág-check ng é-mail** mah·kah·pahg·chehk nahng ee·mehyl
– print	**– makapág-print** mah·kah·pahg·preent
How much per (half) hour?	**Magkáno sa báwat (kalaháting) óras?** mahg·kah·noh sah bah·waht (kah·lah·hah·teeng) oh·rahs
How do I…?	**Paáno ko…?** pah·ah·noh koh…
– connect/disconnect	**– makáka-connéct/magdí-disconnéct** mah·kah·kah·koh·nehkt/mahg·dee·dees·koh·nehkt
– log *on/off*	**– maglá-log *on/off*** mahg·lah·lahg ohn/ohf
– type this symbol	**– magta-týpe ng símbolong itó** mahg·tah·tahyp nahng seem·boh·lohng ee·toh
What's your e-mail?	**Anó ang inyóng é-mail?** ah·noh ahng een·yohng ee·mehyl
My e-mail is…	**Ang é-mail ko ay…** ahng ee·mehyl koh ahy…

You May See...

CLOSE	close
DELÉTE	delete
É-MAIL	e-mail
ÉXIT	exit
HELP	help
ÍNSTANT MÉSSENGER	instant messenger
ÍNTERNET	internet
LÓG-IN	log-in
ON/OFF	on/off
I ÓPEN	open
PRINT	print
SAVE	save
SEND	send
ÚSERNAME/PÁSSWORD	username/password
WÍRELESS ÍNTERNET	wireless internet

Phone

A *phone card/prepaid phone*, please.	**Isáng *phone card/prépaid phone*, please.** ee·<u>sahng</u> fohn kahrd/<u>pree</u>·pehyd fohn plees
How much?	**Magkáno?** mahg·<u>kah</u>·noh
Can I *recharge/buy minutes for* this phone?	**Pwéde ba akóng *magrechárge ng/bumilí ng load pára sa* teléponóng itó?** <u>pweh</u>·deh bah ah·<u>kohng</u> mahg·reh·<u>chahrj</u>·nahng/ boo·mee·<u>lee</u> nahng lohwd <u>pah</u>·rah sah teh·<u>leh</u>·poh·<u>nohng</u> ee·<u>toh</u>
Where's the pay phone?	**Saán ang pay phone?** sah·<u>ahn</u> ahng pehy fohn

My phone doesn't work here.	**Hindî gumagána ang teléponó ko díto.** heen·*dee*' goo·mah·*gah*·nah ahng teh·leh·poh·*noh* koh *dee*·toh
What's the *area/ country* code for…?	**Anó ang *área/cóuntry* code ng…?** ah·*noh* ahng *ehy*·ree·yah/*kahn*·tree kohwd nahng…
What's the number for Information?	**Anó ang número sa ímpormasyón?** ah·*noh* ahng *noo*·meh·roh sah eem·pohr·mah·*shohn*
I'd like the number for…	**Gustó kong humingî ng número ng…** goos·*toh* kohng hoo·mee·*ngee*' nahng *noo*·meh·*roh* nahng…
I'd like to call collect [reverse the charges].	**Gustó kong tumáwag ng colléct.** goos·*toh* kohng too·*mah*·wahg nahng koh·*lehkt*
Can I have your number?	**Pwéde ko bang makúha ang inyóng número?** pweh·deh koh bahng mah·*koo*·hah ahng een·*yohng* *noo*·meh·*roh*
Here's my number.	**Éto ang número ko.** *eh*·toh ahng *noo*·meh·*roh* koh

▶ For numbers, see page 181.

Please *call/text* me.	***Pakitawágan/Pakitéxt* mo akó.** pah·kee·tah·*wah*·gahn/pah·kee·*tehxt* moh ah·*koh*
I'll *call/text* you.	***Tatawágan/Itétext* kitá.** tah·tah·*wah*·gahn/ ee·*teh*·tehkst kee·*tah*

On the Phone

Hello. This is…	**Helló. Si…itó.** heh·*loh* see…ee·*toh*
Can I speak to…?	**Pwéde ko bang makaúsap si…?** pweh·deh koh bahng mah·kah·*oo*·sahp see…
Extension…	**Eksténsiyon…** ehks·tehn·see·*yohn*…
Speak *louder/more slowly*, please.	***Pakilakasán/Pakibagálan* lang ang pagsásalitâ.** pah·kee·lah·kah·*sahn*/ pah·kee·bah·*gah*·lahn lahng ahng pahg·*sah*·sah·lee·*tah*'

Can you repeat that?	**Pwéde ba ninyóng ulítin iyón?** pweh·deh bah neen·<u>yohng</u> oo·<u>lee</u>·teen ee·<u>yohn</u>
I'll call back later.	**Tatáwag akó mamayâ.** tah·<u>tah</u>·wahg ah·<u>koh</u> mah·mah·<u>yah</u>'
Bye.	**Bye.** bahy

Síno ang tumatáwag? <u>see</u>·noh ahng too·mah·<u>tah</u>·wahg	Who's calling?
Pakihintáy lámang. pah·kee·heen·<u>tahy</u> lah·mahng	Hold on.
Walâ siyá díto. wah·<u>lah</u>' see·<u>yah</u> <u>dee</u>·toh	He/She is not here.
Nása kabiláng línya siyá. <u>nah</u>·sah kah·bee·<u>lahng</u> <u>leen</u>·yah see·<u>yah</u>	He/She is on another line.
Gustó nyó bang mag-íwan ng mensáhe? goos·<u>toh</u> <u>nyoh</u> bahng mahg·<u>ee</u>·wahn nahng mehn·<u>sah</u>·heh	Would you like to leave a message?
Pwéde ba nyá kayóng matawágan? <u>pweh</u>·deh bah <u>nyah</u> kah·<u>yohng</u> mah·tah·<u>wah</u>·gahn	Can he/she call you back?
Anó ang inyóng número? ah·<u>noh</u> ahng een·<u>yohng</u> <u>noo</u>·meh·<u>roh</u>	What's your number?

Fax

Can I *send/receive* a fax here?	**Pwéde ba akóng *magpadalá/ makatanggáp* ng fax díto?** <u>pweh</u>·deh bah ah·<u>kohng</u> *mahg·pah·dah·<u>lah</u>/mah·kah·tahng·<u>gahp</u>* nahng fahx <u>dee</u>·toh
What's the fax number?	**Anó ang número ng fax?** ah·<u>noh</u> ahng <u>noo</u>·meh·<u>roh</u> nahng fahx
Please fax this to…	**Pakifax itó sa…** pah·kee·<u>fahx</u> ee·<u>toh</u> sah…

Trying to make a call from a public phone can be a little confusing, mainly because there are various phone companies offering several ways of using a public phone. Some phones take only prepaid cards, which you can buy at a kiosk nearby or in malls. Other phones take only coins. To call domestic long distance, dial the area code then the phone number. To call overseas, dial 00 + country code + area code + the number. If you just need to make a local call, try the ever-present **sari-sari** (small convenience stores), which can be found on most street corners. There you can use their local landline for a small fee.

Post Office

Where's the *post office/mailbox [postbox]*?	**Saán ang *post óffice/máilbox*?** sah·ahn ahng *pohst oh·fees/mehyl·bahx*
A stamp for this *postcard/letter* to…	**Sélyo pára sa *póstcard/súlat* sa…** sehl·yoh pah·rah sah *pohst·kahrd/soo·laht* sah…
How much?	**Magkáno?** mahg·kah·noh
Send this package by *mail/registered mail [post]*.	**Pakipadalá ang pakéteng itó by *aírmail/régistered mail*.** pah·kee·pah·dah·lah ahng pah·keh·tehng ee·toh bahy *ehyr·mehyl/reh·jees·tehrd mehyl*
When will it arrive?	**Kailán itó dárating?** kah·ee·lahn ee·toh dah·rah·teeng
A receipt, please.	**Resíbo, please.** reh·see·boh plees

Sagután ang cústoms dèclarátion form.
sah·goo·tahn ahng kohs·tohms
dehk·lah·rehy·shohn fohrm

Fill out the customs
declaration form.

Anó ang halagá? ah·noh ahng hah·lah·gah

What's the value?

Anó ang nása loób? ah·noh ahng nah·sah loo·ohb

What's inside?

Despite some bad publicity in the past, the Philippine Post Office does a good job of getting mail to its intended destination. Post offices operate Mondays to Fridays, 8 a.m. to 5 p.m. Some are open on Saturdays, 8 a.m. to 12 p.m. You can send your letters and packages by air mail, by sea, registered or by express service.

There are also many international courier services operating in the Philippines, and these are a good choice if you need to get your package to its destination quickly.

▼ Food

Eating Out

Essential

Can you recommend a good *restaurant/ bar*?	**Pwéde ba kayóng magrékomendá ng magandáng *réstorán/bar*?** <u>pweh</u>·deh bah kah·<u>yohng</u> mahg·<u>reh</u>·koh·mehn·<u>dah</u> nahng mah·gahn·<u>dahng</u> <u>rehs</u>·toh·<u>rahn</u>/ bahr
Is there *a traditional Filipino/an inexpensive* restaurant nearby?	**Méron bang *authéntic Filipíno/múra* na réstoráng malápit?** meh·rohn bahng *oh·<u>thehn</u>·teek fee·lee·<u>pee</u>·noh/<u>moo</u>·rah* nah <u>rehs</u>·toh·<u>rahng</u> mah·<u>lah</u>·peet
A table for *one/two*, please.	**Mésa pára sa *isá/dalawá*, please.** meh·sah <u>pah</u>·rah sah ee·<u>sah</u>/dah·lah·<u>wah</u> plees
Can we sit…?	**Pwéde ba kamíng umupô…?** <u>pweh</u>·deh bah kah·<u>meeng</u> oo·moo·<u>poh</u>'
– here/there	**– díto/doón** <u>dee</u>·toh/doo·<u>ohn</u>
– outside	**– sa labás** sah lah·<u>bahs</u>
– in a non-smoking area	**– sa non-smóking área** sah nahn·ees·<u>mohw</u>·keeng <u>ehyr</u>·yah
Where's the restroom [toilet]?	**Saán ang CR?** sah·<u>ahn</u> ahng see·ahr
A menu, please.	**Menú, please.** meh·<u>noo</u> plees
What do you recommend?	**Anó ang inyóng mairerékomendá?** ah·<u>noh</u> ahng een·<u>yohng</u> mah·ee·reh·<u>reh</u>·koh·mehn·<u>dah</u>
I'd like…	**Gustó ko ng…** goos·<u>toh</u> koh nahng…
Some more…, please.	**Dagdagán mo pa ng…, please.** dahg·dah·<u>gahn</u> moh pah nahng…plees
Enjoy your meal!	**Sána mágustuhán ninyó ang pagkáin!** <u>sah</u>·nah <u>mah</u>·goos·too·<u>hahn</u> neen·<u>yoh</u> ahng pahg·<u>kah</u>·een

The check [bill], please.	**Ang bill, please.** ahng beel plees
Is service included?	**Kasáma ba ang sérvice?** kah·<u>sah</u>·mah bah ahng <u>sehr</u>·vees
Can I pay by *credit card/have a receipt*?	**Pwéde ba akóng *magbáyad ng crédit card/makakúha ng resíbo*?** <u>pweh</u>·deh bah ah·<u>kohng</u> *mahg·<u>bah</u>·yahd nahng <u>kreh</u>·deet·kahrd/ mah·kah·<u>koo</u>·hah nahng reh·<u>see</u>·boh*
Thank you!	**Salámat!** sah·<u>lah</u>·maht

Restaurant Types

Can you recommend…?	**Pwéde ba kayóng magrékomendá…?** <u>pweh</u>·deh bah kah·<u>yohng</u> mahg·<u>reh</u>·koh·mehn·<u>dah</u>…
– a restaurant	**– ng réstorán** nahng <u>rehs</u>·toh·<u>rahn</u>
– a bar	**– ng bar** nahng bahr
– a café	**– ng café** nahng kah·<u>fehy</u>
– a fast-food place	**– ng fast food** nahng fahst food

i

Philippine cuisine offers many possibilities, reflecting the diversity of the Filipino people. Filipinos have had contact with foreign cultures for over a thousand years, resulting in a fascinating melding of flavors with the local fare. Spanish and Chinese cooking in particular have greatly influenced Philippine cuisine.

Filipinos are early risers so breakfast starts as early as 6 a.m. Popular breakfast fare includes various kinds of meat such as: **tápa** (tangy dried beef), **lóngganísa** (Philippine sausage) and fried **bangús** (milkfish), all served with a fried egg and rice. For an alternative breakfast, try the ubiquitous **pándesál**, small loaves of salt bread available at any bakery or grocery store and best eaten hot. A good complement to the **pándesál** is some fresh tropical fruit such as yellow mango, pineapple, papaya, banana or watermelon.

Lunch generally begins at noon, while dinner begins anytime after 6 p.m. Dishes for these meals are often interchangeable. Common meals include fried fish, chicken or pork **adóbo** (vinegar and soy sauce broth mixed with garlic, peppercorns, bay leaf and potatoes), **calderéta** (goat stew), **pinakbét** (mixed vegetables of bitter melon, okra, eggplants, squash, string beans and tomatoes), **chop suey** (stir-fried mixed vegetables) and one of the Filipinos' favorite dishes, **sinigang**, a stew of meat or seafood with vegetables cooked in a sour tamarind broth. Barbeque is also very popular throughout the country. As with nearly every meal, rice is served in large quantities.

Popular desserts include fruit, **léche flan** (milk and caramel custard) and **halo-halò** (a mixture of sweetened beans and fruit on top of crushed ice with evaporated milk and/or ice cream).

Merienda (snacks) are served twice a day, once in the late morning and the other at around 3 p.m. Try **kakanín** (rice cakes), **champorádo** (a dish of slightly sweetened rice porridge cooked with chocolate), **bibíngka** (a rice-flour cake often garnished with salted eggs and/or milk cheese), **pansít** (fried noodles garnished with chicken, shrimp and vegetables) or **mámi** (noodle soup with meat and vegetables).

Reservations and Questions

I'd like to reserve a table…	**Gustó kong magparesérba ng mésa…** goos·<u>toh</u> kohng mahg·pah·reh·<u>sehr</u>·bah nahng <u>meh</u>·sah…
– for two	**– pára sa dalawá** <u>pah</u>·rah sah dah·lah·<u>wah</u>
– for this evening	**– pára mámayang gabí** <u>pah</u>·rah <u>mah</u>·mah·yahng gah·<u>bee</u>
– for tomorrow at…	**– pára búkas nang…** <u>pah</u>·rah <u>boo</u>·kahs nahng…
A table for two, please.	**Mésa pára sa dalawá, please.** <u>meh</u>·sah <u>pah</u>·rah sah dah·lah·<u>wah</u> plees
We have a reservation.	**Méron kamíng resérbasyón.** <u>meh</u>·rohn kah·<u>meeng</u> reh·<u>sehr</u>·bah·<u>shohn</u>
My name is…	**…ang pangálan ko.** …ahng pah·<u>ngah</u>·lahn koh
Can we sit…?	**Pwéde ba kamíng umupô…?** <u>pweh</u>·deh bah kah·<u>meeng</u> oo·moo·<u>poh</u>'…
– here/there	**– díto/doón** <u>dee</u>·toh/doo·<u>ohn</u>
– outside	**– sa labás** sah lah·<u>bahs</u>
– in a non-smoking area	**– sa non-smóking área** sah nahn·ees·<u>mohw</u>·keeng <u>ehyr</u>·yah
– in a private dining area	**– sa prívate room** sah <u>prahy</u>·vehyt room
– by the window	**– sa tabí ng bintanà** sah tah·<u>bee</u> nahng been·<u>tah</u>·nah'
Where's the restroom [toilet]?	**Saán ang CR?** sah·<u>ahn</u> ahng see·ahr

You May Hear...

Méron ba kayóng resérbasyón?
<u>meh</u>·rohn bah kah·<u>yohng</u>
reh·<u>sehr</u>·bah·shohn

Do you have
a reservation?

Pára sa ilán? <u>pah</u>·rah sah ee·<u>lahn</u>

How many?

Sa smóking o non-smóking?
sah ees·<u>mohw</u>·keeng oh
nahn·ees·<u>mohw</u>·keeng

Smoking or
non-smoking?

Anó pô ang gustó nilá?
ah·<u>noh</u> poh' ahng goos·<u>toh</u> nee·<u>lah</u>

What would you like?

Inirerékomendá ko pô ang...
ee·nee·reh·<u>reh</u>·koh·mehn·<u>dah</u>
koh poh' ahng...

I recommend...

Sána mágustuhán ninyó ang pagkáin.
<u>sah</u>·nah <u>mah</u>·goos·too·<u>hahn</u>
neen·<u>yoh</u> ahng pahg·<u>kah</u>·een

Enjoy your meal.

Ordering

Waiter/Waitress!	**Wéyter ♂/Wéytres ♀!** <u>wehy</u>·tehr ♂/<u>wehy</u>·trehs ♀
We're ready to order.	**Gustó na náming mag-órder.** goos·<u>toh</u> nah <u>nah</u>·meeng mahg·<u>ohr</u>·dehr
The wine list, please.	**Ang listáhan ng álak, please.** ahng lees·<u>tah</u>·hahn nahng <u>ah</u>·lahk plees
I'd like...	**Gustó ko...** goos·<u>toh</u> koh...
– a bottle of...	**– ng isáng bóte ng...** nahng ee·<u>sahng</u> <u>boh</u>·teh nahng...
– a liter of...	**– ng isáng lítro ng...** nahng ee·<u>sahng</u> <u>lee</u>·troh nahng...
– a glass of...	**– ng isáng báso ng...** nahng ee·<u>sahng</u> <u>bah</u>·soh nahng...

▶ For alcoholic and non-alcoholic drinks, see page 84.

The menu, please.	**Menú, please.** meh-<u>noo</u> plees
Do you have a menu in English/ a fixed-price menu?	**Méron ba kayóng menú sa *Inglés/na nakalagáy ang présyo*?** meh-rohn bah kah-<u>yohng</u> meh-<u>noo</u> sah *eeng-<u>lehs</u>/nah nah-kah-lah-<u>gahy</u> ahng <u>preh</u>-shoh*
What do you recommend?	**Anó ang inyóng mairerékomendá?** ah-<u>noh</u> ahng een-<u>yohng</u> mah-ee-reh-<u>reh</u>-koh-mehn-<u>dah</u>
What's this?	**Anó itó?** ah-<u>noh</u> ee-<u>toh</u>
What's in it?	**Anó ang sahóg nitó?** ah-<u>noh</u> ahng sah-hohg nee-<u>toh</u>
It's to go [take away].	**Take out.** tehyk ahwt

You May See…

MENÚ (SA ÁRAW NA ITÓ)	menu (of the day)
SÉRVICE (HINDÎ) KASÁMA	service (not) included
MGÁ ESPESYÁL NA PAGKÁIN	specials

Cooking Methods

baked	**binéyk** bee-<u>nehyk</u>
boiled/stewed	**nilagà** nee-<u>lah</u>-gah'
blanched	**binanli-án** bee-nahn-lee-<u>ahn</u>
braised	**pinakulubán** pee-nah-koo-loo-<u>bahn</u>
diced	**diced** dahyst
filleted	**filéy** fee-<u>lehy</u>
fried	**príto** <u>pree</u>-toh
grilled	**iníhaw** ee-<u>nee</u>-hahw

poached	**pinakuluán** pee·nah·koo·loo·<u>ahn</u>
roasted	**binusá** bee·noo·<u>sah</u>
sautéed	**ginisá** gee·nee·<u>sah</u>
smoked	**pinausúkan** pee·nah·oo·<u>soo</u>·kahn
steamed	**pinasingawán** pee·nah·see·ngah·<u>wahn</u>
stuffed	**relyéno** rehl·<u>yeh</u>·noh

Special Requirements

Is it *halal/kosher*?	***Halál/Kósher ba yan?*** hah·<u>lahl</u>/<u>koh</u>·shehr bah yahn
I'm...	**Akó ay...** ah·<u>koh</u> ahy...
– diabetic	**– may diabétes** mahy jah·<u>beh</u>·tehs
– lactose intolerant	**– dî pwéde ng may gátas** <u>dee</u>' pweh·deh nahng mahy <u>gah</u>·tahs
– vegetarian	**– végetárian** <u>veh</u>·jeh·<u>tahr</u>·yahn
I'm allergic to...	**May állergy akó sa...** mahy <u>ah</u>·lehr·jee ah·<u>koh</u> sah...
I can't eat...	**Hindî akó pwédeng kumáin...** heen·<u>dee</u>' ah·<u>koh</u> <u>pweh</u>·dehng koo·<u>mah</u>·een...
– dairy	**– ng gawâ sa gátas** nahng gah·<u>wah</u>' sah <u>gah</u>·tahs
– gluten	**– ng glútin** nahng <u>gloo</u>·teen
– nuts	**– ng nuts** nahng nahts
– pork	**– ng karnéng báboy** nahng kahr·<u>nehng</u> <u>bah</u>·bohy
– shellfish	**– ng shéllfish** nahng <u>shehl</u>·feesh
– spicy food	**– ng maangháng na pagkáin** nahng mah·ahng·<u>hahng</u> nah pahg·<u>kah</u>·een
– wheat	**– ng trígo** nahng <u>tree</u>·goh

Dining with Kids

Do you have children's portions?	**Méron ba kayóng sérvings pára sa mgá batà?** meh·rohn bah kah·yohng sehr·veengs pah·rah sah mah·ngah bah·tah'
A *highchair/child's seat*, please.	**Highchair/Upúan pára sa batà**, please. hahy·chehyr/oo·poo·ahn pah·rah sah bah·tah' plees
Where can I *feed/change* the baby?	**Saán ko pwédeng *pakaínin/palitán* ang báby?** sah·ahn koh pweh·dehng pah·kah·ee·neen/ pah·lee·tahn ahng behy·bee
Can you warm this?	**Pwéde ba ninyóng inítin itó?** pweh·deh bah neen·yohng ee·nee·teen ee·toh

▶ For travel with children, see page 156.

Complaints

How much longer will our food be?	**Gaáno katagál pa ba kamíng maghíhintáy ng áming pagkáin?** gah·ah·noh kah·tah·gahl pah bah kah·meeng mahg·hee·heen·tahy nahng ah·meeng pahg·kah·een
We can't wait any longer.	**Hindî na kamí makapaghíhintáy pa.** heen·dee' nah kah·mee mah·kah·pahg·hee·heen·tahy pah
We're leaving.	**Áalís na kamí.** ah·ah·lees nah kah·mee
I didn't order this.	**Hindî ko inórder itó.** heen·dee' koh ee·nohr·dehr ee·toh
I ordered…	**Ang inórder ko ay…** ahng ee·nohr·dehr koh ahy…
I can't eat this.	**Hindî ko pwédeng kaínin itó.** heen·dee' koh pweh·dehng kah·ee·neen ee·toh
This is too…	**Itó ay masyádong…** ee·toh ahy mah·shah·dohng…
– cold/hot	**– malamíg/maínit** mah·lah·meeg/ mah·ee·neet

This is too…	**Itó ay masyádong…** ee·<u>toh</u> ahy mah·<u>shah</u>·dohng…
– salty/spicy	**– maálat/maangháng** mah·<u>ah</u>·laht/ mah·ahng·<u>hahng</u>
– tough/bland	**– matigás/matabáng** mah·tee·<u>gahs</u>/ mah·tah·<u>bahng</u>
This isn't *clean/fresh*.	**Itó ay hindî *malínis/sariwà*.** ee·<u>toh</u> ahy heen·<u>dee</u>' mah·<u>lee</u>·nees/sah·<u>ree</u>·wah'

Paying

The check [bill], please.	**Ang bill, please.** ahng beel plees
Separate checks [bills], please.	**Hiwaláy na bill, please.** hee·wah·<u>lahy</u> nah beel plees
It's all together.	**Magkákasáma lahát.** mahg·<u>kah</u>·kah·<u>sah</u>·mah lah·<u>haht</u>
Is service included?	**Kasáma ba ang sérvice charge?** kah·<u>sah</u>·mah bah ahng <u>sehr</u>·vees chahrj
What's this amount for?	**Pára saán ang halagáng itó?** pah·rah sah·<u>ahn</u> ahng hah·lah·<u>gahng</u> ee·<u>toh</u>
Can I have *a receipt/ an itemized bill*?	**Pwéde ba akóng humingî ng *resíbo/ nakadetálye na bill*?** <u>pweh</u>·deh bah ah·<u>kohng</u> hoo·mee·<u>ngee</u>' nahng *reh·<u>see</u>·boh/ nah·kah·deh·<u>tahl</u>·yeh nah beel*
That was delicious!	**Ang saráp!** ahng sah·<u>rahp</u>

Be sure to check your bill carefully to see if a service charge has been included. Restaurants will usually tack on 10% to your total bill. Value-added tax (VAT) of 12% may also be added. As a general rule, you don't have to tip if a service charge has been included by the establishment. If not, anywhere from 5%–10% of the bill will suffice.

Market

Where are the *carts* [*trolleys*]/*baskets*?	**Saán ang mgá *carts/báskets*?** sah·<u>ahn</u> ahng mah·<u>ngah</u> kahrts/<u>bahs</u>·kets
Where is…?	**Saán ang…?** sah·<u>ahn</u> ahng…

▶ For food items, see page 90.

I'd like some of *that/this*.	**Gustó ko ng kontì *nyán/nitó*.** goos·<u>toh</u> koh nahng kohn·tee' *nyahn/nee·<u>toh</u>*
Can I taste it?	**Pwéde ko bang tikmán?** <u>pweh</u>·deh koh bahng teek·<u>mahn</u>
I'd like…	**Gustó ko…** goos·<u>toh</u> koh…
– a *kilo/half-kilo* of…	– **ng *isáng kílo/kaláhating kílo* ng…** nahng *ee·<u>sahng</u> <u>kee</u>·loh/kah·lah·<u>hah</u>·teeng <u>kee</u>·loh* nahng…
– a liter of…	– **ng isáng lítro ng…** nahng ee·<u>sahng</u> <u>lee</u>·troh nahng…
– a piece of…	– **ng isáng piráso ng…** nahng ee·<u>sahng</u> pee·<u>rah</u>·soh nahng…
– a slice of…	– **ng isáng hiwà ng…** nahng ee·<u>sahng</u> <u>hee</u>·wah' nahng…
More/Less.	**Humigít/Kumúlang.** hoo·mee·<u>geet</u>/koo·<u>moo</u>·lahng
How much?	**Magkáno?** mahg·<u>kah</u>·noh
Where do I pay?	**Saán akó magbabáyad?** sah·<u>ahn</u> ah·<u>koh</u> mahg·bah·<u>bah</u>·yahd
I'm being helped.	**Tinútulungan akó.** tee·<u>noo</u>·too·loo·ngahn ah·<u>koh</u>

▶ For conversion tables, see page 186.

Pwéde ko ba kayóng tulúngan? pweh·deh koh bah kah·yohng too·loo·ngahn	Can I help you?
Anó ang inyóng gustó? ah·noh ahng een·yohng goos·toh	What would you like?
Anó pa? ah·noh pah	Anything else?
Iyán ay…píso. ee·yahn ahy…pee·soh	That's…pesos.

With their breathtaking array of vegetables, fruit, meat, seafood and general food items, traditional **paléngkes** (open-air markets) offer an enticing feast for the senses. Metro Manila abounds with markets of all types offering nearly everything under the sun; these are open daily from early morning and some until midnight.

Manila's biggest market for food is Divisoria, in the San Nicolas section of the old city. Many hotels, restaurants, neighborhood markets, as well as businesses of all types, obtain their goods from Divisoria. Another popular market is the Baclaran Flea Market, along Roxas Boulevard in Baclaran, Parañaque, which sells food, flowers and household items. The San Andres Market in Malate, Manila offers an eye-catching display of tropical fruit. The Seaside Market in Baclaran sells fresh seafood, which one can have prepared by any of the adjoining restaurants for a reasonable fee. In Quezon City, the massive Balintawak food market is similar in scope to Divisoria and is open 24 hours. Also fun to check out in Quezon City is the Farmer's Market Cubao and Nepa-Q Mart near Kamias. Traditional air-conditioned supermarkets can be found in most cities in the country and many offer excellent variety and pleasant surroundings. Prices here would normally be about 10%–20% higher than in the **paléngke**.

You May See...

GAMÍTIN BÁGO...	best if used by...
CÁLORIES	calories
WALÁNG TABÂ	fat-free
PANATILÍING NAKARÉFRIGERÁTOR	keep refrigerated
ITINDÁ BÁGO...	sell by...
WALÁNG ASÚKAL	sugar-free
BÁGAY SA MGÁ VÉGETÁRIAN	suitable for vegetarians

Dishes, Utensils and Kitchen Tools

bottle opener	**pambukás ng bóte** pahm·boo·<u>kahs</u> nahng <u>boh</u>·teh
bowl	**mangkók** mahng·<u>kohk</u>
can opener	**ábre-láta** <u>ahb</u>·reh·<u>lah</u>·tah
corkscrew	**córkscrew** <u>kohrk</u>·skroo
cup	**tása** <u>tah</u>·sah
fork	**tinidór** tee·nee·<u>dohr</u>
frying pan	**kawalì** kah·<u>wah</u>·lee'
glass	**báso** <u>bah</u>·soh
(steak) knife	**kutsílyo (pára sa stéak)** koo·<u>cheel</u>·yoh (<u>pah</u>·rah sah ees·<u>tehyk</u>)
measuring cup/spoon	**measuring cup/spoon** <u>meh</u>·shoo·reeng kahp/spoon
napkin	**nápkin** <u>nahp</u>·keen
plate	**pláto** <u>plah</u>·toh
pot	**kaldéro** kahl·<u>deh</u>·roh
spatula	**espátula** ehs·<u>pah</u>·too·lah
spoon	**kutsára** koo·<u>chah</u>·rah

Meals

Breakfast

bácon <u>behy</u>·kohn — bacon

(*malamíg/maínit* na) céreal (cold/hot) cereal
(mah·lah·<u>meeg</u>/mah·ee·neet nah) <u>seer</u>·yahl

gátas <u>gah</u>·tahs — milk

hótdog <u>haht</u>·dohg — hotdog

...itlóg ...eet·<u>lohg</u> — ...egg

– hard-boiled/malasádong — *hard-/soft*-boiled
<u>hahrd</u>·bohyld/mah·lah·<u>sah</u>·dohng

– prítong <u>pree</u>·tohng — – fried

– maálat na mah·<u>ah</u>·laht nah — – salted

– binatí na bee·nah·<u>tee</u> nah — – scrambled

– súnny side up na <u>sah</u>·nee sahyd ahp nah — – sunny side up

jam/jélly jahm/<u>jeh</u>·lee — jam/jelly

...juice ...joos — ...juice

– ápple <u>ah</u>·pohl — – apple

– grape grehyp — – grape

– órange <u>oh</u>·rehynj — – orange

– pineápple pahyn·<u>ah</u>·pohl — – pineapple

kapé/tsaá... kah·<u>peh</u>/chah·<u>ah</u>... — coffee/tea...

– na waláng asúkal at kréma nah — – black
wah·<u>lahng</u> ah·<u>soo</u>·kahl aht <u>kreh</u>·mah

I'd like...	**Gustó ko ng...** goos·<u>toh</u> koh nahng...
More... please.	**Dagdagán mo pa ng..., please.** dahg·dah·<u>gahn</u> moh pah nahng...plees

– **decáf** deh·_kahf_   – decaf

– **may gátas** mahy _gah_·tahs   – with milk

– **may asúkal** mahy ah·_soo_·kahl   – with sugar

– **may artificial _swéetener/Équal_**® mahy _ahr_·tee·_fee_·shahl _swee_·teh·nehr/ _ee_·kwahl   – with _artificial sweetener/Equal_®

késo _keh_·soh   cheese

mantekílya mahn·teh·_keel_·yah   butter

márgarín _mahr_·gah·_reen_   margarine

óatmeal _ohwt_·meel   oatmeal

páncake _pahn_·kehyk   pancake

sinangág see·nah·_ngahg_   rice fried with garlic

soríso soh·_ree_·soh   Chinese or Spanish sausage

tápa _tah_·pah   dried meat

tinápay tee·_nah_·pahy   bread (loaf)/roll

tocíno toh·_see_·noh   cured meat

tórta _tohr_·tah   omelet

tostádo tohs·_tah_·doh   toast

tsokoláte choh·koh·_lah_·teh   chocolate drink

túbig _too_·beeg   water

tuyô too·_yoh_'   dried fish

yógart _yoh_·gahrt   yogurt

With/Without…	**Mérong/Waláng…** _meh_·rohng/wah·_lahng_…
I can't have…	**Hindî akó pwédeng may…** heen·_dee_' ah·_koh_ _pweh_·dehng mahy…

Soup

la paz bátchoy lah pahz baht·<u>chohy</u>	noodle soup with pork craklings, vegetables and egg
bulalô boo·lah·<u>loh</u>'	beef and bone marrow soup
nilágang báka nee·<u>lah</u>·gahng <u>bah</u>·kah	beef soup with potatoes and cabbage
sabáw ng manók sah·<u>bahw</u> nahng mah·<u>nohk</u>	chicken soup
sinigáng see·nee·<u>gahng</u>	a sour soup of pork or seafood
tomáto soup toh·<u>mehy</u>·toh soop	tomato soup
végetable soup <u>vehj</u>·tah·bohl soop	vegetable soup

Fish and Seafood

alimángo ah·lee·<u>mah</u>·ngoh	mud crab
alimásag ah·lee·<u>mah</u>·sahg	blue crab
apáhap ah·<u>pah</u>·hahp	sea bass
bagoóng bah·goh·<u>ohng</u>	shrimp paste
bának <u>bah</u>·nahk	mullet
bangús bah·<u>ngoos</u>	milkfish
dílis <u>dee</u>·lees	anchovy
espáda ehs·<u>pah</u>·dah	swordfish
gíndará <u>geen</u>·dah·<u>rah</u>	cod

I'd like…	**Gustó ko ng…** goos·<u>toh</u> koh nahng…
More… please.	**Dagdagán mo pa ng…, please.** dahg·dah·<u>gahn</u> moh pah nahng…plees

hípon hee·pohn		shrimp
hitò hee·toh'		catfish
lápulápu lah·poo·lah·poo		grouper
mákarel mah·kah·rehl		mackerel
pusít poo·seet		squid
salmón sahl·mohn		salmon
séaweed see·weed		seaweed
tahóng tah·hohng		mussels
talabá tah·lah·bah		oyster
tilápya tee·lah·pyah		tilapia
tulyá tool·yah		clam
túna too·nah		tuna

With/Without…	**Mérong/Waláng…** meh·rohng/wah·lahng…
I can't have…	**Hindî akó pwédeng may…** heen·dee' ah·koh pweh·dehng mahy…

i The rich assortment of fish and shellfish in the Philippines makes seafood an important part of the Filipino diet. **Bangús** (milkfish), **tilápya** (tilapia) and **hitò** (catfish) are some of the common freshwater fish. They can be prepared in different ways, but the most common is by frying or grilling, then serving them with a light soy sauce and slices of fresh tomatoes. These are priced much lower than saltwater fish such as tuna, salmon and cod. Many deep-sea fish are served as grilled steaks or used in soup with leafy vegetables. Other seafood such as clams, shrimp, squid, crabs, oysters and seaweed are always abundant and fresh. While elegant dishes abound for shellfish, they are usually simply steamed and enjoyed from the shell. **Adóbong pusit** is squid cooked in soy sauce, vinegar and its own black ink. Seaweed, meanwhile, can be mixed with diced onions and tomatoes and dressed with vinegar for a simple yet delicious salad.

Meat and Poultry

atáy ah·tahy	liver
bácon behy·kohn	bacon
hamón hah·mohn	ham
kambíng kahm·beeng	goat
karnéng báboy kahr·nehng bah·bohy	pork
karnéng báka kahr·nehng bah·kah	beef
karnéng kalabáw kahr·nehng kah·lah·bahw	water buffalo meat
kuného koo·neh·hoh	rabbit
manók mah·nohk	chicken
pábo pah·boh	turkey

I'd like…	**Gustó ko ng…** goos·toh koh nahng…
More…, please.	**Dagdagán mo pa ng…, please.** dahg·dah·gahn moh pah nahng…plees

páto pah·toh		duck
soríso soh·ree·soh		Chinese or Spanish sausage
stéak ees·tehyk		steak
tupà too·pah'		lamb

rare	**dî gaánong lutô** dee' gah·ah·nohng loo·toh'
medium	**katamtáman ang pagkalutò** kah·tahm·tah·mahn ahng pahg·kah·loo·toh'
well-done	**lutúng-lutô** loo·toong·loo·toh'

Vegetables and Staples

ampalayá ahm·pah·lah·yah	bitter gourd
básil behy·seel	basil
báwang bah·wahng	garlic
beans beens	beans
brokóli broh·koh·lee	broccoli
cárrot kah·roht	carrot
cauliflówer koh·lee·flah·wehr	cauliflower
green beans green beens	green beans
kabuté kah·boo·teh	mushroom
kalabása kah·lah·bah·sah	squash
kamátis kah·mah·tees	tomato
kangkóng kahng·kohng	swamp cabbage
kánin kah·neen	rice

With/Without…	**Mérong/Waláng…** meh·rohng/wah·lahng…
I can't have…	**Hindî akó pwédeng may…** heen·dee' ah·koh pweh·dehng mahy…

labanós lah·bah·<u>nohs</u>	radish
labóng lah·<u>bohng</u>	bamboo shoots
laurél lahw·<u>rehl</u>	bay leaf
letsúgas leht·<u>soo</u>·gahs	lettuce
lúya <u>loo</u>·yah	ginger
maís mah·<u>ees</u>	corn
malunggáy mah·loong·<u>gahy</u>	horseradish
mustása moos·<u>tah</u>·sah	mustard
ókra <u>ohk</u>·rah	okra
oréganó oh·<u>reh</u>·gah·<u>noh</u>	oregano
párseley <u>pahrs</u>·lee	parsley
pásta <u>pahs</u>·tah	pasta
patátas pah·<u>tah</u>·tahs	potato
pétsay <u>peh</u>·chahy	Chinese cabbage
pusò ng ságing <u>poo</u>·soh' nahng <u>sah</u>·geeng	banana heart
repólyo reh·<u>pohl</u>·yoh	cabbage
séleri <u>seh</u>·leh·ree	celery
sibúyas see·<u>boo</u>·yahs	onion
síling *pulá/bérde* <u>see</u>·leeng *poo·<u>lah</u>/<u>be hr</u>·deh*	*red/green* pepper
sítaw <u>see</u>·tahw	string beans
sitsaró see·chah·<u>roh</u>	snow peas
spínach ees·<u>pee</u>·nahch	spinach
talóng tah·<u>lohng</u>	eggplant [aubergine]
úbe <u>oo</u>·beh	yam

I'd like...	**Gustó ko ng...** goos·<u>toh</u> koh nahng...
More... please.	**Dagdagán mo pa ng..., please.** dahg·dah·<u>gahn</u> moh pah nahng...plees

Fruit

abokádo ah·boh·<u>kah</u>·doh		avocado
átis <u>ah</u>·tees		sugar apple
bayábas bah·<u>yah</u>·bahs		guava
dáyap <u>dah</u>·yahp		lime
dúhat <u>doo</u>·haht		Java plum
durián door·<u>yahn</u>		durian
guyabáno goo·yah·<u>bah</u>·noh		soursop
kasúy kah·<u>sooy</u>		cashew nut
kaymíto kahy·<u>mee</u>·toh		star apple
langkâ lahng·<u>kah</u>'		jackfruit
lansónes lahn·<u>soh</u>·nehs		lanzones
mabólo mah·<u>boh</u>·loh		mabolo
makópa mah·<u>koh</u>·pah		rose apple
manggá mang·<u>gah</u>		mango
mángostéen <u>mang</u>·gohs·<u>teen</u>		mangosteen
mansánas mahn·<u>sah</u>·nahs		apple
melón meh·<u>lohn</u>		melon
órange <u>oh</u>·rehynj		orange
pakwán pahk·<u>wahn</u>		watermelon
papáya pah·<u>pah</u>·yah		papaya
pinyá peen·<u>yah</u>		pineapple
plum plahm		plum

With/Without…	**Mérong/Waláng…** <u>meh</u>·rohng/wah·<u>lahng</u>…
I can't have…	**Hindî akó pwédeng may…** heen·<u>dee</u>' ah·<u>koh</u> <u>pweh</u>·dehng mahy…

ságing sah·geeng	banana
santól sahn·tohl	sandor fruit (santol)
sinigwélas see·neeg·weh·lahs	Spanish plum
stráwberry ees·troh·beh·ree	strawberry
suhà soo·hah'	pomelo
tsésa cheh·sah	chesa
tsíko chee·koh	chico
úbas oo·bahs	grape

A wide selection of tropical fruit is always available in the Philippines. The Philippine **manggá** (mango) is famous for its luscious golden flesh. It is eaten fresh, pureed into shakes and juices, used as filling for crepes and pastries, or dried and candied. **Ságing** (banana) and **pinyá** (pineapple) are not only enjoyed as freshly picked fruit but also used in desserts and stews. Less well-known but equally delectable are the large, elongated **langkâ** (jackfruit), with coarse yellow-green skin enclosing sweet, yellow flesh; **lansónes**, egg-shaped fruit in bunches, with light brown skin and translucent flesh; the round **mángostéen**, delicious white flesh encased in a tough purple skin; the **suhà** (pomelo), resembling a large grapefruit with a thick yellow or pink rind, inside which are sweet segments that may contain a hint of tartness; and the **átis** (sugar apple), a palm-sized fruit with scaly gray-green skin, which is pressed open at one end to reveal the white segments within. The **átis** can be difficult to eat because of the many seeds, but the soft, sugary segments are well worth the effort.

I'd like…	**Gustó ko ng…** goos·toh koh nahng…
More… please.	**Dagdagán mo pa ng…, please.** dahg·dah·gahn moh pah nahng…plees

Dessert

bagkát na *ságing/kamóte* bahg·<u>kaht</u> nah <u>sah</u>·geeng/kah·<u>moh</u>·teh
banana/sweet potato in thick, sweet sauce

banána/maís con hiélo bah·<u>nah</u>·nah/ mah·<u>ees</u> kohn <u>yeh</u>·loh
banana/corn topped with ice, milk and caramelized sugar

búko pandán <u>boo</u>·koh pahn·<u>dahn</u>
diced pine-flavored gelatin with coconut strips in thick cream

ginataáng halo-halò gee·nah·tah·<u>ahng</u> hah·loh·<u>hah</u>·loh'
sweetened assorted tropical fruit in thick coconut cream

halayáng úbe hah·lah·<u>yahng</u> <u>oo</u>·beh
yam sweetened with sugar and margarine

halo-halò hah·loh·<u>hah</u>·loh'
a variety of sweetened fruit topped with crushed ice and custard

kakanín kah·kah·<u>neen</u>
sweetened glutinous rice in coconut oil and wrapped in banana leaves

léche flan <u>leh</u>·cheh flahn
milk and caramel custard

makapunô sweets mah·kah·poo·<u>noh</u>' sweets
coconut meat rolled in sugar and milk

péanut bríttle <u>pee</u>·naht <u>bree</u>·tehl
peanuts in caramelized sugar

With/Without…	**Mérong/Waláng…** <u>meh</u>·rohng/wah·<u>lahng</u>…
I can't have…	**Hindî akó pwédeng may…** heen·<u>dee</u>' ah·<u>koh</u> <u>pweh</u>·dehng mahy…

pastíllas de léche pahs·<u>teel</u>·yahs deh <u>leh</u>·cheh	soft and creamy milk candy wrappedin paper
pastíllas de *langkâ/úbe* pahs·<u>teel</u>·yahs *deh lahng·<u>kah</u>' /<u>oo</u>·beh*	jackfruit-/yam-flavored milk candy wrapped in paper
sapín-sapín sah·<u>peen</u>·sah·<u>peen</u>	sweetened rice cake
yéma <u>yeh</u>·mah	peanut crunch

Drinks

Essential

The *wine list/drink menu*, please.	**Ang *listáhan ng álak/drink menú*, please.** ahng lees·<u>tah</u> hanh nahng <u>ah</u>·lahk/dreengk meh·<u>noo</u> plees
What do you recommend?	**Anó ang inyóng mairerékomendá?** ah·<u>noh</u> ahng een·<u>yohng</u> mah·ee·reh·<u>reh</u>·koh·mehn·dah
I'd like a *bottle/glass* of *red/white* wine.	**Gustó ko ng isáng *bóte/báso* ng álak na *red/white*.** goos·<u>toh</u> koh nahng ee·<u>sahng</u> <u>boh</u>·teh/<u>bah</u>·soh nahng <u>ah</u>·lahk nah *red/wahyt*
The house wine, please.	**Ang house wine, please.** ahng hahws wahyn plees
Another *bottle/glass*, please.	**Isá pang *bóte/báso*, please.** ee·<u>sah</u> pahng <u>boh</u>·teh/<u>bah</u>·soh plees
I'd like a local beer.	**Gustó ko ng lokál na beer.** goos·<u>toh</u> koh nahng loh·<u>kahl</u> nah beer
Can I buy you a drink?	**Pwéde ba kitáng ibilí ng inúmin?** <u>pweh</u>·deh bah kee·<u>tahng</u> ee·bee·lee·<u>lee</u> nahng ee·<u>noo</u>·meen
Cheers!	**Cheers!** cheers

A *coffee/tea*, please.	***Kapé/Tsaá*, please.** kah·*peh*/chah·*ah* plees
With…	**May…** mahy…
– milk	**– gátas** <u>gah</u>·tahs
– sugar	**– asúkal** ah·<u>soo</u>·kahl
– artificial sweetener/ Equal®	**– artifícial swéetener/Équal®** ahr·tee·<u>fee</u>·shahl <u>swee</u>·teh·nehr/<u>ee</u>·kwahl
A *juice/soda*, please.	***Juice/Softdrink*, please.** joos/sohft·dreengk plees
Is the water safe to drink?	**Ókey bang inumín ang túbig?** <u>oh</u>·kehy bahng ee·noo·<u>meen</u> ahng <u>too</u>·beeg

Non-alcoholic Drinks

frappé frah·<u>pehy</u>	a frozen drink or thick milk shake
gátas <u>gah</u>·tahs	milk
iced tea ahys tee	iced tea
juice joos	juice
kapé kah·<u>peh</u>	coffee
lemonáda leh·moh·<u>nah</u>·dah	lemonade
maínit na tsokoláte mah·<u>ee</u>·neet nah choh·koh·<u>lah</u>·te	hot chocolate
soft drinks <u>sohft</u> dreengks	soda
(míneral/distílled na) túbig (<u>mee</u>·neh·rahl/<u>dees</u>·<u>teeld</u> nah) <u>too</u>·beeg	(mineral/distilled) water

As one might expect in a tropical country brimming with exotic fruit, the Philippines is an excellent place for lovers of fresh fruit juices and shakes. Most restaurants offer ripe yellow mango shake, green mango shake, **búko** (young coconut) juice, **dalandán** (native green orange) juice and **calamansí** (native lemon) juice. Fruit shake stands can be found at most malls. A popular way to enjoy **búko** is by sipping the cool coconut water inside the shell through a straw, after which the shell is cracked open and the tender flesh scooped out and enjoyed. Coconut vendors ply the streets in old wooden carts stacked with green coconuts. Just approach them and ask them for fresh **búko**. Watching them deftly cut up the coconut with their sharp **bólo** knife is almost as enjoyable as drinking the succulent juice inside.

For non-fruit-based drinks, one can try **sagó at guláman**, a mildly sweet drink made of water mixed with syrup, **sagó** (tapioca balls) and gelatin cubes.

Tahó is a thick, protein-rich drink made of soft tofu, syrup and **sagó**, served warm. It is usually sold by vendors early in the mornings. **Tahó** vendors carry two large metal drums over their shoulders and shout "tahooooo" into the air. **Tahó** and **sagó at guláman** can also be found in restaurants offering Filipino cuisine.

You May Hear...

Pwéde ba kitáng ikúha ng inúmin? pweh·deh bah kee·tahng ee·koo·hah nahng ee·noo·meen	Can I get you a drink?
May gátas o asúkal? mahy gah·tahs oh ah·soo·kahl	With milk or sugar?
Túbig gáling sa gripo, míneral, o distílled wáter? too·beeg gah·leeng sah gree·poh oh mee·neh·rahl oh dees·teeld woh·tehr	Tap, mineral or distilled water?

Aperitifs, Cocktails and Liqueurs

brándy brahn·dee	brandy
gin jeen	gin
rum rahm	rum
scótch ees·kahch	scotch
tequíla teh·kee·lah	tequila
vódka vohd·kah	vodka
whísky wees·kee	whisky

Beer

beer... beer... ...beer

- **sa bóte/na draft** sah boh·teh/nah drahft – bottled/draft
- **na *dark/light*** nah dahrk/lahyt – dark/light
- **na pale pílsen** nah pehyl peel·sehn – pale pilsner
- **na *lokál/impórted*** nah loh·kahl/ – local/imported
  eem·pohr·tehd
- **na waláng álkohol** nah wah·lahng – non-alcoholic
  ahl·koh·hol

San Miguel Corporation is the oldest and largest brewery in the Philippines, with facilities even in other Asian countries and in Australia. The most popular beer is San Miguel® Pale Pilsen, a pilsner with a light, crisp, refreshing taste. San Mig Light™ has fewer calories. San Miguel also brews Cerveza Negra, a dark beer with a creamy consistency and bitter taste. Asia Brewery Inc. is San Miguel's strongest competitor. Its flagship product Beer na Beer® has a smooth, clean taste and costs less than San Miguel® beer. Other beer products under Asia Brewery include Colt 45®, Carlsberg® and Lone Star®.

Wine

álak... ah·lahk... ...wine

- **na *dry/sweet*** nah drahy/sweet – dry/sweet
- **na manggá** nah mahng·gah – mango
- **na *red/white*** nah rehd/wahyt – red/white
- **na spárkling** nah spahr·kleeng – sparkling
- **na stráwberry** nah ees·troh·beh·ree – strawberry

– **na tápuy** nah <u>tah</u>·pooy — rice

– **na tubâ** nah too·<u>bah</u>' — coconut

– **na lambanóg** nah lahm·bah·<u>nohg</u> — distilled coconut

house/táble **wine** hahws/<u>tehy</u>·bohl wayn — *house/table* wine

champágne chahm·<u>pehyn</u> — champagne

Different types of wine are produced in the Philippines using tropical plants and fruit, such as coconut palms and mangoes. **Tubâ** (coconut wine) is tapped from the crown of the coconut palm and drunk fresh or fermented. Distilled coconut wine is called **lambanóg** and has higher alcohol content. The making of **tápuy** (rice wine) is filled with suspense, for only after the six-month-long fermentation process can one know if it is drinkable or not. Fruit wine, such as mango and strawberry wine, bears the fragrant scent of the fruit used. Ripe mango wine has a pleasant, well-rounded flavor. Green mango wine has a crisp, clear taste and a tart aroma.

Menu Reader

abokádo ah·boh·<u>kah</u>·doh — avocado

adóbo ah·<u>doh</u>·boh — pork, chicken or vegetable cooked in vinegar, soy sauce, garlic, peppercorns and bay leaf

álak <u>ah</u>·lahk — wine

alimángo ah·lee·<u>mah</u>·ngoh — crab

alimásag ah·lee·<u>mah</u>·sahg — blue crab

ampalayá ahm·pah·lah·<u>yah</u> — bitter gourd

apáhap ah·<u>pah</u>·hahp — sea bass

arróz cáldo ah·<u>rohz</u> <u>kahl</u>·doh — rice soup with chicken, peppercorns and ginger, topped with browned garlic

ártichoke <u>ahr</u>·tee·chohwk — artichoke

artifícial swéetener ahr·tee·fee·shahl <u>swee</u>·teh·nehr — artificial sweetener

asín ah·<u>seen</u> — salt

aspáragus ahs·<u>pah</u>·rah·goos — asparagus

asúkal ah·<u>soo</u>·kahl — sugar

atáy ah·<u>tahy</u> — liver

átis <u>ah</u>·tees — sugar apple

atsára ah·<u>chah</u>·rah — pickle

bácon <u>behy</u>·kohn — bacon

bagoóng bah·goh·<u>ohng</u> — shrimp paste

báka <u>bah</u>·kah — ox

balíkat bah·<u>leeh</u>·kaht — shoulder

balút bah·<u>loot</u> — boiled, fertilized duck egg

bának <u>bah</u>·nahk — mullet

banána cue bah·<u>nah</u>·nah kyoo — fried bananas with caramelized sugar served on skewers

bangús bah·<u>ngoos</u> — milkfish

básil <u>behy</u>·seel — basil

báwang <u>bah</u>·wahng — garlic

bayábas bah·<u>yah</u>·bahs — guava

bean been — bean

beer beer — beer

beet beet — beet

bibíngka bee·<u>beeng</u>·kah — rice-flour cake topped with salted egg and/or cheese

brándy brahn·dee	brandy
brázo de mercédes brah·zoh deh mehr·seh·dehs	meringue cake
brokóli broh·koh·lee	broccoli
bukayò boo·kah·yoh'	sweetened coconut meat
bulalô boo·lah·loh'	beef with bone marrow soup
buntót ng báka boon·toht nahng bah·kah	oxtail
búttermilk bah·tehr·meelk	buttermilk
cake kehyk	cake
camarón rebosádo kah·mah·rohn reh·boh·sah·doh	deep-fried shrimp
cáper kehy·pehr	caper
cárrot kah·roht	carrot
cauliflówer koh·lee·flah·wehr	cauliflower
céreal seer·yahl	cereal
champorádo chahm·poh·rah·doh	rice porridge with chocolate
chúrros choo·rohs	deep-fried bread dipped in chocolate
cínnamón see·nah·mohn	cinnamon
cookie koo·kee	cookie [biscuit]
córnmeal kohrn·meel	cornmeal
crácker krah·kehr	cracker
cream cheese kreem chees	cream cheese
dáing dah·eeng	salted and dried fish that has been split open

dalanghíta dah·lahng·<u>hee</u>·tah	tangerine
dáyap <u>dah</u>·yahp	lime
decáf deh·<u>kahf</u>	decaf
dilà <u>dee</u>·lah'	tongue
diláw dee·<u>lahw</u>	turmeric
dílis <u>dee</u>·lees	anchovy
dinuguán dee·noo·goo·<u>ahn</u>	pork mixed with blood and vinegar
dóughnut <u>doh</u>·naht	doughnut
dúhat <u>doo</u>·haht	Java plum
dúmpling <u>dahmp</u>·leeng	dumpling
durián door·<u>yahn</u>	durian; a prickly-skinned fruit with a pungent odor
émbutído <u>ehm</u>·boo·<u>tee</u>·doh	rolled ground pork
énsaláda ehn·sah·<u>lah</u>·dah	salad
énsaymáda ehn·sahy·<u>mah</u>·dah	bread topped with margarine and sugar
Équal® <u>ee</u>·kwahl	Equal®
éskabéche <u>ehs</u>·kah·<u>beht</u>·cheh	fish sautéed in spices
espáda ehs·<u>pah</u>·dah	swordfish
fig feeg	fig
fish balls feesh bohls	fish rolled into balls and dipped in sweet sauce
french fries frehnch frahys	french fries
frítter <u>free</u>·tehr	fritter
gábi <u>gah</u>·bee	taro

gansâ gahn·<u>sah</u>'	goose
gatâ gah·<u>tah</u>'	coconut milk
gátas <u>gah</u>·tahs	milk
gin jeen	gin
gíndará <u>geen</u>·dah·<u>rah</u>	cod
gisántes gee·<u>sahn</u>·tehs	peas
granáda grah·<u>nah</u>·dah	pomegranate
gúlay <u>goo</u>·lahy	vegetable
guyabáno goo·yah·<u>bah</u>·noh	soursop; a thorny fruit with fibrous flesh, usually made into juice
hálibút <u>hah</u>·lee·<u>boot</u>	halibut
halo-halò hah·loh <u>hah</u>·loh'	a variety of sweetened fruit topped with crushed ice and custard
hámburger <u>hahm</u>·bohr·gehr	hamburger
hamón hah·<u>mohn</u>	ham
hípon <u>hee</u>·pohn	shrimp
hitò <u>hee</u>·toh'	catfish
hótdog <u>haht</u>·dohg	hotdog
ice cube ahys kyoob	ice cube
ígat <u>ee</u>·gaht	eel
inahíng manók ee·nah·<u>heeng</u> mah·<u>nohk</u>	hen
iníhaw na báka ee·<u>nee</u>·hahw nah <u>bah</u>·kah	grilled beef
isdâ ees·<u>dah</u>'	fish
isdáng lapád ees·<u>dahng</u> lah·<u>pahd</u>	sole
itlóg eet·<u>lohg</u>	egg

jam jahm	jam
jélly <u>jeh</u>·lee	jelly
juice joos	juice
kabuté kah·boo·<u>teh</u>	mushroom
kakáng gatâ kah·<u>kahng</u> gah·<u>tah</u>'	coconut cream
kakanín kah·kah·<u>neen</u>	sweetened sticky rice
kalabása kah·lah·<u>bah</u>·sah	squash
kalderéta kahl·deh·<u>reh</u>·tah	pork, beef, water buffalo or goat meat cooked with tomato sauce
kamátis kah·<u>mah</u>·tees	tomato
kambíng kahm·<u>beeng</u>	goat
kamóte kah·<u>moh</u>·teh	sweet potato
kamyás kahm·<u>yahs</u>	sour fruit used in stews
kangkóng kahng·<u>kohng</u>	swamp cabbage
kánin <u>kah</u>·neen	rice
kapé kah·<u>peh</u>	coffee
káramel <u>kah</u>·rah·mehl	caramel
kare-karé kah·reh·kah·<u>reh</u>	vegetables and beef with peanut sauce
kárne <u>kahr</u>·neh	meat
kárne nórte <u>kahr</u>·neh <u>nohr</u>·teh	corned beef
karnéng báboy kahr·<u>nehng</u> <u>bah</u>·bohy	pork
karnéng báka kahr·<u>nehng</u> <u>bah</u>·kah	beef
karnéng tupà kahr·<u>nehng</u> <u>too</u>·pah'	mutton
karnéng usá kahr·<u>nehng</u> oo·<u>sah</u>	venison

kastányas kas·<u>tahn</u>·yahs	chestnut
kasúy kah·<u>sooy</u>	cashew nut
kaymíto kahy·<u>mee</u>·toh	star apple
kéndi <u>kehn</u>·dee	candy [sweets]
késo <u>keh</u>·soh	cheese
késo de bóla <u>keh</u>·soh deh <u>boh</u>·lah	special round cheese for Christmas
késong putî <u>keh</u>·sohng poo·<u>tee</u>'	cottage cheese
kétsap <u>keht</u>·chahp	ketchup
kídney <u>keed</u>·nee	kidney
kilawín kee·lah·<u>ween</u>	meat, fish or vegetable seasoned with vinegar
kíwi <u>kee</u>·wee	kiwi
klábo <u>klah</u>·boh	clove
kréma <u>kreh</u>·mah	cream
kulántro koo·<u>lahn</u>·troh	cilantro [coriander]
kuného koo·<u>neh</u>·hoh	rabbit
kutsínta koo·<u>cheen</u>·tah	sweetened sticky rice cake
kwék-kwek <u>kwehk</u>·kwehk	fried quail eggs
labanós lah·bah·<u>nohs</u>	radish
labóng lah·<u>bong</u>	bamboo shoots
lamán ng alimángo lah·<u>mahn</u> nahng ah·lee·<u>mah</u>·ngoh	crabmeat
lamáng loób lah·<u>mahng</u> loo·<u>ohb</u>	innards
lamáng loób ng báka lah·<u>mahng</u> loo·<u>ohb</u> nahng <u>bah</u>·kah	tripe

langkâ lahng·<u>kah</u>' jackfruit

lansónes lahn·<u>soh</u>·nehs lanzones; egg-shaped fruit in small bunches

lápulápu <u>lah</u>·poo·<u>lah</u>·poo grouper

laurél lahw·<u>rehl</u> bay leaf

léche flan <u>leh</u>·cheh flahn milk and caramel custard

lechón leh·<u>chohn</u> roasted whole pig, chicken, or beef

lechón de léche leh·<u>chohn</u> deh <u>leh</u>·cheh roasted whole suckling pig

leek leek leek

lémon <u>leh</u>·mohn lemon

lemonáda leh·moh·<u>nah</u>·dah lemonade

léngua estofáda <u>lehng</u>·gwah ehs·toh·<u>fah</u>·dah ox tongue stew

lentéhas lehn·<u>teh</u>·hahs lentils

letsúgas leht·<u>soo</u>·gahs lettuce

liémpo <u>lyehm</u>·poh grilled pork with skin and some layers of fat

lómi <u>loh</u>·mee large noodles in thick sauce

lómo <u>loh</u>·moh sirloin

lóngganísa <u>lohng</u>·gah·<u>nee</u>·sah Philippine sausage

lúgaw <u>loo</u>·gahw rice porridge

lúmpia <u>loom</u>·pyah spring roll; vegetables and/or meat rolled in egg wrapper

lúya <u>loo</u>·yah	ginger
mabólo mah·<u>boh</u>·loh	mabolo; a hairy, dark red fruit
makapunô mah·kah·poo·<u>noh</u>'	coconut meat
maís mah·<u>ees</u>	corn
mákarel <u>mah</u>·kah·rehl	mackerel
makaróni mah·kah·<u>roh</u>·nee	macaroni
makópa mah·<u>koh</u>·pah	rose apple
malunggáy mah·loong·<u>gahy</u>	horseradish
mámi <u>mah</u>·mee	noodle soup with meat and vegetables
manggá mahng·<u>gah</u>	mango
mángostéen <u>mang</u>·gohs·<u>teen</u>	mangosteen; a round purple fruit with sweet white flesh
maní mah·<u>nee</u>	peanuts
manók mah·<u>nohk</u>	chicken
mansánas mahn·<u>sah</u>·nahs	apple
mantekílya mahn·teh·<u>keel</u>·yah	butter
manúkan mah·<u>noo</u>·kahn	poultry
márgarín <u>mahr</u> gah·<u>reen</u>	margarine
marmaláda mahr·mah·<u>lah</u>·dah	marmalade
máyonnaise <u>mah</u>·yoh·neys	mayonnaise
mechádo meh·<u>chah</u>·doh	beef or pork cooked in tomato sauce
melón meh·<u>lohn</u>	melon
menúdo meh·<u>noo</u>·doh	pork or chicken with red pepper, potatoes and tomato sauce

meréngge meh·<u>rehng</u>·geh	meringue
minatamís mee·nah·tah·<u>mees</u>	sweets
mint meent	mint
misó mee·<u>soh</u>	soybean cake
munggó moong·<u>goh</u>	mung beans
mustása moos·<u>tah</u>·sah	mustard
niyóg nee·<u>yohg</u>	coconut
nútmeg <u>naht</u>·mehg	nutmeg
nuts nahts	nuts
óatmeal <u>ohwt</u>·meel	oatmeal
ókra <u>ohk</u>·rah	okra
ólive <u>oh</u>·leev	olive
ólive oil <u>oh</u>·leev ohyl	olive oil
oréganó oh·<u>reh</u>·gah·<u>noh</u>	oregano
paá pah·<u>ah</u>	leg
pábo <u>pah</u>·boh	turkey
paélya pah·<u>ehl</u>·yah	rice mixed with seafood, meat and vegetables
paksíw pahk·<u>seew</u>	fish or meat cooked with vinegar and garlic
pakwán pahk·<u>wahn</u>	watermelon
palitáw pah·lee·<u>tahw</u>	boiled rice cake with grated coconut
pamintá pah·meen·<u>tah</u>	ground black pepper (seasoning)
pámpasaráp <u>pahm</u>·pah·sah·<u>rahp</u>	spices
pámpatamís <u>pahm</u>·pah·tah·<u>mees</u>	sweetener

páncake pahn·keyk	pancake
pandán pahn·dahn	leaves of the screw pine used to flavor desserts
pándesál pahn·deh·sahl	small loaves of salt bread
pangá ng túna pah·ngah nahng too·nah	grilled meaty jaw part of tuna
panghimágas pahng·hee·mah·gahs	dessert
pansít pahn·seet	fried noodles garnished with chicken, shrimp and vegetables
papáya pah·pah·yah	papaya
páprika pah·pree·kah	paprika
pársley pahrs·lee	parsley
pásas pah·sahs	raisin
pásta pahs·tah	pasta
pastíllas de léche pahs·teel·yahs deh leh·cheh	soft and creamy milk candy wrapped in paper
pástry pehys·tree	pastry
patátas pah·tah·tahs	potato
paté pah·tehy	paté
páto pah·toh	duck
peach peech	peach
pécho (ng manók) peh·choh (nahng mah·nohk)	breast (of chicken)
péras peh·rahs	pear
pétsay peh·chahy	Chinese cabbage

phéasant feh·sahnt — pheasant

pie pahy — pie

píli pee·lee — a nut found in the Bicol region

pináis pee·nah·ees — shrimp and coconut wrapped in banana leaves

pinakbét pee·nahk·beht — vegetables seasoned with shrimp paste

pinaupóng manók pee·nah·oo·pohng mah·nohk — steamed chicken with herbs

pinyá peen·yah — pineapple

pipíno pee·pee·noh — cucumber

pízza peet·sah — pizza

pólborón pohl·boh·rohn — confection of flour with powdered milk and sugar

potchéro poht·cheh·roh — a stew of meat, vegetables and banana slices

prune proon — prune

prútas proo·tas — fruit

pugíta poo·gee·tah — octopus

pugò poo·goh' — quail

pulá ng itlóg poo·lah nahng eet·lohg — egg yolk

pulút poo·loot — honey

pulútan poo·loo·tahn — finger food

pusít poo·seet — squid

pusò poo·soh' — heart

pusò ng ságing poo·soh' nahng sah·geeng — banana heart

putî ng itlóg poo-<u>teeh</u>' nahng eet-<u>lohg</u>	egg white
púto bumbóng <u>poo</u>-toh boom-<u>bohng</u>	violet rice steamed in bamboo poles
raspbérry rahsp-<u>beh</u>-ree	raspberry
relyéno rehl-<u>yeh</u>-noh	stuffed fish or seafood
repólyo reh-<u>pohl</u>-yoh	cabbage
repólyong pulá reh-<u>pohl</u>-yohng poo-<u>lah</u>	red cabbage
rum rahm	rum
sa malamíg sah mah-lah-<u>meeg</u>	a cold beverage
sabáw sah-<u>bahw</u>	soup/broth
sabáw ng manók sah-<u>bahw</u> nahng mah-<u>nohk</u>	chicken soup
sáfron <u>sah</u>-frohn	saffron
sage sehyj	sage
ságing <u>sah</u>-geeng	banana
salabát sah-lah-<u>baht</u>	ginger tea
salámi sah-<u>lah</u>-mee	salami
salmón sahl-<u>mohn</u>	salmon
sándwich <u>sahnd</u>-weech	sandwich
santól sahn-<u>tohl</u>	sandor fruit (santol); a round yellow-orange fruit
sapín-sapín sah-<u>peen</u>-sah-<u>peen</u>	sweetened rice cake made of multicolored rice flour and assembled in layers
sardínas sahr-<u>dee</u>-nahs	sardine
sársa <u>sahr</u>-sah	sauce
scállop ees-<u>kah</u>-lohp	scallop
scótch ees-<u>kahch</u>	scotch

séafood see·food	seafood
séleri seh·leh·ree	celery
shawárma shah·wahr·mah	chicken or beef placed in pita bread
shéllfish shehl·feesh	shellfish
shérry sheh·ree	sherry
sibúyas see·boo·yahs	onion
sídra seed·rah	cider
síli see·lee	pepper (vegetable)
sinampalúkang manók see·nahm·pah·loo·kahng mah·nohk	chicken in tamarind broth
sinangág see·nah·ngahg	rice fried with garlic
síngkamas seeng·kah·mahs	turnip
sinigáng see·nee·gahng	a sour stew of pork or seafood
sinigwélas see·neeg·weh·lahs	Spanish plum
sírup see·roop	syrup
sísig see·seeg	meat or seafood in sizzling hot plate
sítaw see·tahw	string beans
sitsaró see·chah·roh	snow peas
sitsarón seet·sah·rohn	a crispy snack from pork, beef or water buffalo skin
sóftdrink sohft·dreengk	soda
sorbétes sohr·beh·tehs	ice cream
soríso soh·ree·soh	Chinese or Spanish sausage
sóya soh·yah	soy [soya]

sóya milk <u>soh</u>·yah meelk	soymilk [soya milk]
spaghétti ees·pah·<u>geh</u>·tee	spaghetti
spínach ees·<u>pee</u>·nahch	spinach
stéak ees·<u>tehyk</u>	steak
stráwberry ees·<u>troh</u>·beh·ree	strawberry
suhà <u>soo</u>·hah'	pomelo; a citrus fruit similar to grapefruit
sukà <u>soo</u>·kah'	vinegar
súman <u>soo</u>·mahn	rice cake wrapped in banana or palm leaves
susô soo·<u>soh</u>'	snail
sweet and sour sauce sweet ahnd sahwr sohs	sweet and sour sauce
sweet corn sweet kohrn	sweet corn
tahó tah·<u>hoh</u>	soybean drink with caramelized sugar
tahóng tah·<u>hohng</u>	mussel
talabá tah·lah·<u>bah</u>	oyster
talóng tah·<u>lohng</u>	eggplant [aubergine]
tamáles tah·<u>mah</u>·lehs	cake made of powdered rice
tápa <u>tah</u>·pah	dried meat
tárragon <u>tah</u>·rah·gohn	tarragon
thyme thahym	thyme
tilápya tee·<u>lah</u>·pyah	tilapia
tinadtád na kárne tee·nahd·<u>tahd</u> nah <u>kahr</u>·neh	chopped meat
tinapá tee·nah·<u>pah</u>	smoked fish
tinápay tee·<u>nah</u>·pahy	bread (loaf)/roll

tinólang manók tee·noh·lahng mah·nohk — chicken cooked with vegetables, chili leaves and garlic

tocíno toh·see·noh — cured meat

tófu toh·foo — tofu

tóge toh·geh — bean sprouts

tókwa tohk·wah — soybean curd

tórta tohr·tah — omelet

tostádo tohs·tah·doh — toast

toyò toh·yoh' — soy sauce

trígo tree·goh — wheat

tsaá tsah·ah — tea

tsésa cheh·sah — chesa; a plum-like fruit

tsíko chee·koh — chico; a hairy brown fruit with soft, sweet flesh

tsokoláte choh·koh·lah·teh — chocolate

túbig too·beeg — water

tulyá tool·yah — clam

túna too·nah — tuna

tupà too·pah' — lamb

túpig too·peeg — rice cake wrapped in banana leaves

turón too·rohn — banana fritters in thin flour wrappers

tuyô too·yoh' — dried fish

úbas oo·bahs — grapes

úbe oo·beh — yam

úbod oo·bohd	core of the coconut tree
úkoy oo·kohy	vegetable and seafood patty
úlang oo·lahng	lobster
útaw oo·tahw	soybean [soya bean]
vanílya vah·neel·yah	vanilla
vódka vohd·kah	vodka
wálnut wahl·naht	walnut
whip cream weep kreem	whipped cream
whísky wees·kee	whisky
yérba yehr·bah	herb
yógart yoh·gahrt	yogurt

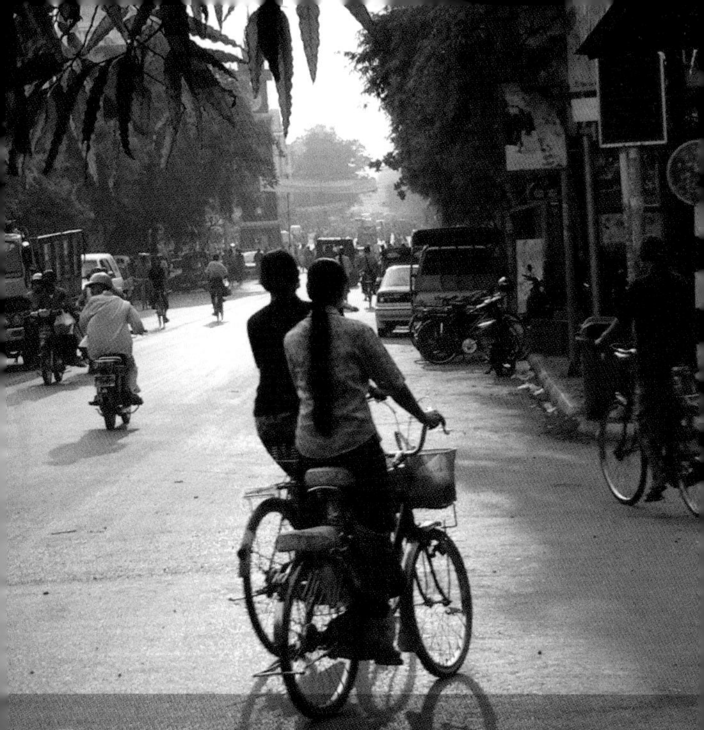

People

Talking

Essential

Hello!	**Helló!** heh·<u>loh</u>
Hi!	**Hi!** hahy
How are you?	**Kumustá kayó?** koo·moos·<u>tah</u> kah·<u>yoh</u>
Fine, thanks.	**Mabúti namán, salámat.** mah·<u>boo</u>·tee nah·<u>mahn</u> sah·<u>lah</u>·maht
Excuse me!	**Mawaláng gálang nga pô!** mah·wah·<u>lahng</u> <u>gah</u>·lahng ngah <u>poh</u>'
Do you speak English?	**Nagsásalitâ ba kayó ng Inglés?** nahg·<u>sah</u>·sah·lee·<u>tah</u>' bah kah·<u>yoh</u> nahng eeng·<u>lehs</u>
What's your name?	**Anó ang inyóng pangálan?** ah·<u>noh</u> ahng een·<u>yohng</u> pah·ngah·lahn
My name is…	**…ang pangálan ko.** …ahng pah·<u>ngah</u>·lahn koh
Nice to meet you.	**Ikinagágalák kong makilála kayó.** ee·kee·nah·<u>gah</u>·gah·<u>lahk</u> kohng mah·kee·<u>lah</u>·lah kah·<u>yoh</u>
Where are you from?	**Taga saán kayó?** tah·gah sah·<u>ahn</u> kah·<u>yoh</u>
I'm from the U.S./U.K.	**Taga *U.S./U.K.* akó.** tah·gah *<u>yoo</u>·ehs/<u>yoo</u>·kehy* ah·<u>koh</u>
What do you do?	**Anó ang inyóng trabáho?** ah·<u>noh</u> ahng een·<u>yohng</u> trah·<u>bah</u>·hoh
I work for…	**Nagtátrabáho akó sa…** nahg·<u>tah</u>·trah·<u>bah</u>·hoh ah·<u>koh</u> sah…
I'm a student.	**Estudyánte akó.** ehs·tood·<u>yahn</u>·teh ah·<u>koh</u>
I'm retired.	**Retirádo na akó.** reh·tee·<u>rah</u>·doh nah ah·<u>koh</u>

Do you like...?	**Gustó ba ninyó ng...?** goos·toh bah neen·yoh nahng...
Goodbye.	**Bye.** bahy
See you later.	**Magkíta táyo mamayâ.** mahg·kee·tah tah·yoh mah·mah·yah'

i Respect, politeness, tact—these traits are nurtured in Filipinos from childhood and show in the choice of words used to address different people. Elders are always shown deference, and Filipinos use certain words when addressing parents, older brothers and sisters and important individuals. For the traveler, use of words such as "sir" and "ma'am" will be much appreciated. Addressing someone as "Mr.," "Mrs." or "Ms." is also a good idea. Professionals are usually called by their title, such as "Attorney Gonzales" or "Doctor Guzman." A good habit to pick up is using the word **po. Po** is added to show respect to an elder or one in a higher position, as in **salámat po** (thank you).

Communication Difficulties

Do you speak English?	**Nagsásalitâ ba kayó ng Inglés?** nahg·sah·sah·lee·tah' bah kah·yoh nahng eeng·lehs
Does anyone here speak English?	**Méron bang nagsásalitâ díto ng Inglés?** meh·rohn bahng nahg·sah·sah·lee·tah' dee·toh nahng eeng·lehs
I don't speak (much) Filipino.	**Hindî akó (masyádong) nakakapágsalitâ ng Filipíno.** heen·dee' ah·koh (mah·shah·dohng) nah·kah·kah·pahg·sah·lee·tah' nahng fee·lee·pee·noh
Can you speak more slowly?	**Pwéde bang bagálan ninyó ang pagsásalitâ?** pweh·deh bahng bah·gah·lahn neen·yoh ahng pahg·sah·sah·lee·tah'

Can you repeat that?	**Pwéde ba ninyóng úlitin iyón?** <u>pweh</u>·deh bah neen·<u>yohng</u> <u>oo</u>·lee·teen ee·<u>yohn</u>
Excuse me?	**Pakiúlit namán?** pah·kee·<u>oo</u>·leet nah·<u>mahn</u>
What was that?	**Anó iyón?** ah·<u>noh</u> ee·<u>yohn</u>
Can you spell it?	**Pwéde ba ninyóng iispél itó?** <u>pweh</u>·deh bah neen·<u>yohng</u> ee·ees·<u>pehl</u> ee·<u>toh</u>
Please write it down.	**Pakisúlat.** pah·kee·<u>soo</u>·laht
Can you translate this into English for me?	**Pwéde ba ninyóng isálin itó sa Inglés pára sa ákin?** <u>pweh</u>·deh bah neen·<u>yohng</u> ee·<u>sah</u>·leen ee·<u>toh</u> sah eeng·<u>lehs</u> <u>pah</u>·rah sah <u>ah</u>·keen
What does *this/that* mean?	**Anó ang íbig sabíhin *nitó/niyón*?** ah·<u>noh</u> ahng <u>ee</u>·beeg sah·<u>bee</u>·heen *nee·<u>toh</u>/nee·<u>yohn</u>*
I understand.	**Naiintíndihán ko.** nah·ee·een·<u>teen</u>·dee·<u>hahn</u> koh
I don't understand.	**Hindî ko naiintíndihán.** heen·<u>dee</u>' koh nah·ee·een·<u>teen</u>·dee·<u>hahn</u>
Do you understand?	**Naiintíndihán ba ninyó?** nah·ee·een·<u>teen</u>·dee·<u>hahn</u> bah neen·<u>yoh</u>

You May Hear...

Hindî akó masyádong nakakapágsalitâ ng Inglés. heen·<u>dee</u>' ah·<u>koh</u> mah·<u>shah</u>·dohng nah·kah·kah·<u>pahg</u>·sah·lee·<u>tah</u>' nahng eeng·<u>lehs</u>	I only speak a little English.
Hindî akó nakakapágsalitâ ng Inglés. heen·<u>dee</u>' ah·<u>koh</u> nah·kah·kah·<u>pagh</u>·sah·lee·<u>tah</u>' nahng eeng·<u>lehs</u>	I don't speak English.

Making Friends

Hello!	**Helló!** heh·loh
Good morning.	**Magandáng umága.** mah·gahn·dahng oo·mah·gah
Good afternoon.	**Magandáng hápon.** mah·gahn·dahng hah·pohn
Good evening.	**Magandáng gabí.** mah·gahn·dahng gah·bee
My name is…	**…ang pangálan ko.** …ahng pah·ngah·lahn koh
What's your name?	**Anó ang inyóng pangálan?** ah·noh ahng een·yohng pah·ngah·lahn
I'd like to introduce you to…	**Gustó ko kayóng ipakilála kay…** goos·toh koh kah·yohng ee·pah·kee·lah·lah kahy…
Pleased to meet you.	**Ikinagágalák ko na makilála kayó.** ee·kee·nah·gah·gah·lahk koh nah mah·kee·lah·lah kah·yoh
How are you?	**Kumustá kayó?** koo·moos·tah kah·yoh
Fine, thanks. And you?	**Mabúti namán, salámat. At kayó?** mah·boo·tee nah·mahn sah·lah·maht aht kah·yoh

111

i

When it comes to greetings, Filipinos follow both Western and their own cultural norms. A handshake offered by both men and women is a perfectly acceptable form of saying hello and goodbye. Close female friends may greet each other or their colleagues and relatives with a hug or a kiss, or simply by touching cheeks together. You'll often see Filipinos greeting each other by smiling and raising their eyebrows up and down quickly. The traditional way of greeting and showing respect for elders is the **pagmamáno**, or placing the back of the elder person's hand on to the younger person's forehead. This tradition is still widely practiced in small towns and provinces.

Travel Talk

I'm here…	**Nandíto akó…** nahn·<u>dee</u>·toh ah·<u>koh</u>…
– on business	**– pára sa offícial búsiness** pah·rah sah oh·<u>fee</u>·shal <u>bees</u>·nehs
– on vacation [holiday]	**– pára sa bakasyón** pah·rah sah bah·kah·<u>shohn</u>
– studying	**– pára mag-áral** pah·rah mahg·<u>ah</u>·rahl
I'm staying for…	**Manánatíli akó díto hanggáng…** mah·<u>nah</u>·nah·<u>tee</u>·lee ah·<u>koh</u> dee·toh hahng·<u>gahng</u>…
I've been here…	**Nandíto akó noón pang…** nahn·<u>dee</u>·<u>toh</u> ah·<u>koh</u> noh·<u>ohn</u> pahng…
– a day	**– isáng áraw** ee·<u>sahng</u> <u>ah</u>·rahw
– a week	**– isáng linggó** ee·<u>sahng</u> leeng·<u>goh</u>
– a month	**– isáng buwán** ee·<u>sahng</u> boo·<u>wahn</u>

▶ For numbers, see page 181.

Where are you from?	**Taga saán kayó?** tah·gah sah·<u>ahn</u> kah·<u>yoh</u>
I'm from…	**Taga…akó.** tah·gah…ah·<u>koh</u>

Relationships

Who are you with?	**Síno ang kasáma ninyó?** <u>see</u>·noh ahng kah·<u>sah</u>·mah neen·yoh
I'm here alone.	**Mag-isá lang akó díto.** mahg·ee·<u>sah</u> lahng ah·<u>koh</u> <u>dee</u>·toh
I'm with my...	**Kasáma ko ang áking...** kah·<u>sah</u>·mah koh ahng <u>ah</u>·keeng...
– husband/wife	**– asáwa** ah·<u>sah</u>·wah
– boyfriend/girlfriend	**– bóyfriend/gírlfriend** <u>bohy</u>·frehnd/<u>gehrl</u>·frehnd
– brother/sister	**– kapatíd** kah·pah·<u>teed</u>
– mother/father	**– nánay/tátay** <u>nah</u>·nahy/<u>tah</u>·tahy
– friend/colleague	**– kaibígan/kasáma sa trabáho** kah·ee·<u>bee</u>·gahn/kah·<u>sah</u>·mah sa trah·<u>bah</u>·hoh
When's your birthday?	**Kailán ang inyóng bírthday?** kah·ee·<u>lahn</u> ahng een·<u>yohng</u> <u>berth</u>·dehy
How old are you?	**Iláng taón na kayó?** ee·<u>lahng</u> tah·<u>ohn</u> nah kah·<u>yoh</u>
I'm...	**...na akó.** ...nah ah·<u>koh</u>

▶ For numbers, see page 181.

Are you married?	**May asáwa na ba kayó?** mahy ah·<u>sah</u>·wah nah bah kah·<u>yoh</u>
I'm...	**...akó.** ...ah·<u>koh</u>
– single	**– Binatà ♂/Daléga ♀** bee·<u>nah</u>·tah' ♂/dah·<u>lah</u>·gah ♀
– in a relationship	**– May bóyfriend ♂/gírlfriend ♀** mahy <u>bohy</u>·frehnd ♂/<u>gehrl</u>·frehnd ♀
– engaged/married	**– Ikákasal na/May asáwa na** ee·<u>kah</u>·kah·sahl nah/mahy ah·<u>sah</u>·wah nah

I'm…	…akó. …ah·<u>koh</u>
– divorced	– **Diborsyádo** ♂ /**Diborsyáda** ♀ dee·bohr·<u>shah</u>·doh ♂ /dee·bohr·<u>shah</u>·dah ♀
– separated	– **Hiwaláy** hee·wah·<u>lahy</u>
– widowed	– **Biyúdo** ♂ /**Biyúda** ♀ bee·<u>yoo</u>·doh ♂ / bee·<u>yoo</u>·dah ♀
Do you have *children/* *grandchildren*?	**Méron ba kayóng *mgá anák/mgá apó*?** <u>meh</u>·rohn bah kah·<u>yohng</u> mah·ngah ah·<u>nahk</u>/ mah·<u>ngah</u> ah·<u>poh</u>

Work and School

What do you do?	**Anó ang inyóng trabáho?** ah·<u>noh</u> ahng een·<u>yohng</u> trah·bah·hoh
What are you studying?	**Anó ang inyóng pinag-áaralan?** ah·<u>noh</u> ahng een·<u>yohng</u> pee·nahg·<u>ah</u>·ah·rah·lahn
I'm studying Filipino.	**Nag-aáral akó ng Filipíno.** nahg·ah·<u>ah</u>·rahl ah·<u>koh</u> nahng fee·lee·<u>pee</u>·noh
I…	**Akó…** ah·<u>koh</u>…
– work *full-time/ part-time*	– **ay nagtatrabáho ng *fúll-time/párt-time*** ahy nahg·tah·trah·<u>bah</u>·hoh nahng *fool*·tahym/ *pahrt*·tahym
– am unemployed	– **ay waláng trabáho** ahy wah·<u>lahng</u> trah·<u>bah</u>·hoh
– work at home	– **ay nagtatrabáho sa báhay** ahy nahg·tah·trah·<u>bah</u>·hoh sah <u>bah</u>·hahy
Who do you work for?	**Kaninó kayó nagtatrabáho?** kah·nee·<u>noh</u> kah·<u>yoh</u> nahg·tah·trah·<u>bah</u>·hoh
I work for…	**Nagtatrabáho akó sa…** nahg·tah·trah·<u>bah</u>·hoh ah·<u>koh</u> sa…
Here's my business card.	**Etó ang áking búsiness card.** eh·<u>toh</u> ahng <u>ah</u>·keeng <u>bees</u>·nehs kahrd

▶ For business travel, see page 153.

Weather

What's the forecast?	**Anó ang pagtáya ng panahón?** ah·<u>noh</u> ahng pahg·<u>tah</u>·yah nahng pah·nah·<u>hohn</u>
What *beautiful/ terrible* weather!	***Nápakagandá/Nápakasamâ* ng panahón!** *nah·pah·kah·gahn·<u>dah</u>/<u>nah</u>·pah·kah·sah·<u>mah</u>'* nahng pah·nah·<u>hohn</u>
Will it be... tomorrow?	**Búkas kayá ay...?** <u>boo</u>·kahs kah·<u>yah</u> ahy...
– cool/warm	– **mahángin/maínit** mah·<u>hah</u>·ngeen/mah·<u>ee</u>·neet
– cold/hot	– **malamíg/maínit** mah·lah·<u>meeg</u>/mah·<u>ee</u>·neht
– rainy/sunny	– **maulán/maáraw** mah·oo·<u>lahn</u>/mah·<u>ah</u>·rahw
Do I need *a jacket/ an umbrella*?	**Kailángan ko bá ng *jácket/páyong*?** kah·ee·<u>lah</u>·ngahn koh <u>bah</u> nahng *jah·keht/ pah·yohng*

▶ For temperature, see page 187.

Romance

Essential

Would you like to go out for *a drink/dinner*?	**Gustó mo bang lumabás pára *uminóm/ kumáin*?** goos·<u>toh</u> moh bahng loo·mah·<u>bahs</u> pah·rah *oo·mee·<u>nohm</u>/koo·<u>mah</u>·een*
What are your plans for *tonight/tomorrow*?	**Anó ang pláno mo pára *mamayáng gabí/búkas*?** ah·<u>noh</u> ahng <u>plah</u>·noh moh <u>pah</u>·rah *mah·mah·<u>yahng</u> gah·<u>bee</u>/<u>boo</u>·kahs*
Can I have your number?	**Pwéde ko bang makúha ang número ng teléponó mo?** <u>pweh</u>·deh koh bahng mah·<u>koo</u>·hah ahng <u>noo</u>·meh·<u>roh</u> nahng teh·<u>leh</u>·poh·<u>noh</u> moh

Can I join you?	**Pwéde ba kitáng samáhan?** pweh·deh bah kee·tahng sah·mah·hahn
Can I get you a drink?	**Pwéde ba kitáng ikúha ng inúmin?** pweh·deh bah kee·tahng ee·koo·hah nahng ee·noo·meen
I *like/love* you.	*Gustó/Mahál* kitá. goos·toh/mah·hahl kee·tah

Making Plans

Would you like to go out for…?	**Gustó mo bang lumabás pára…?** goos·toh moh bahng loo·mah·bahs pah·rah…
– coffee	**– magkapé** mahg·kah·peh
– a drink	**– uminóm** oo·mee·nohm
– dinner	**– kumáin** koo·mah·een
What are your plans for…?	**Anó ang pláno mo…?** ah·noh ahng plah·noh moh…
– today	**– ngayóng áraw** ngah·yohng ah·rahw
– tonight	**– mámayáng gabí** mah·mah·yahng gah·bee
– tomorrow	**– búkas** boo·kahs
Where would you like to go?	**Saán mo gustóng pumuntá?** sah·ahn moh goos·tohng poo·moon·tah
I'd like to go to…	**Gustó kong pumuntá sa…** goos·toh kohng poo·moon·tah sah…
Do you like…?	**Gustó mo bang…?** goos·toh moh bahng…
Can I have your *number/e-mail*?	**Pwéde ko bang makúha ang *númeró ng teléponó/e-mail* mo?** pweh·deh koh bahng mah·koo·hah ahng noo·meh·roh nahng teh·leh·poh·noh/ee·mehyl moh

▶ For e-mail and phone, see page 53.

Pick-up [Chat-up] Lines

Can I join you?	**Pwéde ba kitáng samáhan?** <u>pweh</u>·deh bah kee·<u>tahng</u> sah·<u>mah</u>·hahn
You're very attractive.	**Nápakagandá mo.** nah·pah·kah·gahn·<u>dah</u> moh
Let's go somewhere quieter.	**Pumuntá táyo sa mas tahímik na lugár.** poo·moon·<u>tah</u> <u>tah</u>·yoh sah mahs tah·<u>hee</u>·meek nah loo·<u>gahr</u>

Accepting and Rejecting

I'd love to.	**Síge, gustó ko.** <u>see</u>·gee goos·<u>toh</u> koh
Where should we meet?	**Saán táyo magkikíta?** sah·<u>ahn</u> <u>tah</u>·yoh mahg·kee·<u>kee</u>·tah
I'll meet you at *the bar/your hotel*.	**Magkíta táyo sa *bar/iyóng hotél*.** mahg·<u>keh</u>·tah <u>tah</u>·yoh sah *bahr/ee·<u>yohng</u> hoh tehl*
I'll come by at…	**Dádatíng akó ng…** <u>dah</u>·dah·<u>teeng</u> ah·<u>koh</u> nahng…

▶ For time, see page 183.

I'm busy.	**Búsy akó.** bee·see ah·koh
I'm not interested.	**Hindî akó interesádo.** heen·dee' ah·koh een·teh·reh·sah·doh
Leave me alone.	**Iwánan mo nga akóng mag-isá.** ee·wah·nahn moh ngah ah·kohng mahg-ee·sah
Stop bothering me!	**Tigílan mo nga ang pang-aabála sa ákin!** tee·gee·lahn moh ngah ahng pahng·ah·ah·bah·lah sah ah·keen

Getting Physical

Can I *hug/kiss* you?	**Pwéde ba kitáng *mayákap/mahalikán?*** pweh·deh bah kee·tahng mah·yah·kahp/ mah·hah·lee·kahn
Yes.	**Óo.** oh·oh
No.	**Hindî.** heen·dee'
Stop!	**Tumígil ka!** too·mee·geel kah
I *like/love* you.	***Gustó/Mahál* kitá.** goos·toh/mah·hal kee·tah

Sexual Preferences

Are you gay?	**Baklâ ka ba?** bahk·lah' kah bah
I'm…	**…akó.** …ah·koh
– heterosexual	– **Hetéroséxual** heh·teh·roh·sehk·swahl
– homosexual	– **Baklâ♂/Tómboy♀** bahk·lah' ♂ /tohm·bohy ♀
– bisexual	– **Biséxual** bahy·sehk·swahl
Do you like *men/women?*	**Gustó mo ba ng mgá *laláki/babáe?*** goos·toh moh bah nahng mah·ngah lah·lah·kee/bah·bah·eh

118

▼ Fun

Sightseeing

Where's the tourist information office?	**Saán ang informátion óffice pára sa mgá turísta?** sah-<u>ahn</u> ahng een-fohr-<u>mehy</u>-shohn <u>oh</u>-fees <u>pah</u>-rah sah mah-<u>ngah</u> too-<u>rees</u>-tah
What are the main attractions?	**Anó ang mgá pángunáhing atraksyón na pwédeng puntahán?** ah-<u>noh</u> ahng mah-<u>ngah</u> pah-ngoo-<u>nah</u>-heeng ah-trahk-<u>shohn</u> nah <u>pweh</u>-dehng poon-tah-<u>hahn</u>
Do you have tours in English?	**May mgá tour ba kayó na Inglés ang gámit na salitâ?** mahy mah-<u>ngah</u> toor bah kah-<u>yoh</u> nah eeng-<u>lehs</u> ahng <u>gah</u>-meet nah sah-lee-<u>tah</u>'
Can I have a *map/guide*?	**Pwéde ba akóng makahingî ng *mápa/ gabáy*?** <u>pweh</u>-deh bah ah-<u>kohng</u> mah-kah-hee- ngee' nahng *<u>mah</u>-pah/gah-<u>bahy</u>*

Tourist Information Office

Do you have information on...?	**May ímpormasyón ba kayó sa...?** mahy <u>eem</u>-pohr-mah-<u>shohn</u> bah kah-<u>yoh</u> sah...
How do we get there?	**Paáno kamí makákapúnta doón?** pah-<u>ah</u>-noh kah-<u>mee</u> mah-<u>kah</u>-kah-<u>poon</u>-tah doh-<u>ohn</u>
Can you recommend...?	**Pwéde ba kayóng magrékomendá...?** <u>pweh</u>-deh bah kah-<u>yohng</u> mahg-<u>reh</u>-koh-mehn-<u>dah</u>...
– a boat trip	**– ng boat trip** nahng bohwt treep
– a bus tour	**– ng bus tour** nahng bahs toor
– an excursion to...	**– ng ékskursiyón sa...** nahng <u>ehks</u>-koor-see-<u>yohn</u> sah...
– a sightseeing tour	**– ng síghtseeing tour** nahng <u>sahyt</u>-<u>see</u>-eeng toor

The Department of Tourism (DOT) website has comprehensive information on Philippine tourism, including the locations of the various DOT offices in cities around the country. Regional offices can be good places to get general information about the area, hotels and resorts, types of transportation on offer and to pick up brochures and maps. Other options to obtain tourist information include visiting local and provincial government websites and offices, and visiting a travel agency.

▶ For useful websites, see page 187.

Tours

I'd like to go on the tour to…	**Gustó kong mag-tour sa…** goos·<u>toh</u> kohng mahg·toor sah…
When's the next tour?	**Kailán ang súsunod na tour?** kah·ee·<u>lahn</u> ahng <u>soo</u>·soo·nohd nah toor
Are there tours in English?	**May mgá tour ba na Inglés ang gámit na salitâ?** mahy mah·<u>ngah</u> toor bah nah eeng·<u>lehs</u> ahng <u>gah</u>·meet nah sah·lee·<u>tah</u>'
Is there an English *guide book/audio guide*?	**May *guide book/audio guide* ba sa Inglés?** mahy *gahyd book/<u>oh</u>·dee·yoh gahyd* bah sah eeng·<u>lehs</u>
I'd like to see…	**Gustó kong makíta ang…** goos·<u>toh</u> kohng mah·<u>kee</u>·tah ahng…
Can we stop here…?	**Pwéde ba tayóng tumígil díto…?** <u>pweh</u>·deh bah tah·<u>yohng</u> too·<u>mee</u>·geel <u>dee</u>·toh…
– to take photos	**– pára kumúha ng retráto** pah·rah koo·<u>moo</u>·hah nahng reht·<u>rah</u>·toh
– for souvenirs	**– pára sa mgá souvenír** pah·rah sah mah·<u>ngah</u>·soo·vee·<u>neer</u>
– for the restrooms [toilets]	**– pára makapág-CR** pah·rah mah·kah·<u>pahg</u> see·ahr

Can we look around?	**Pwéde ba kamíng tumingín-tingín sa palígid?** pweh·deh bah kah·meeng too·mee·ngeen·tee·ngeen sah pah·lee·geed
Is it handicapped [disabled] accessible?	**Madalî ba itóng puntahán ng may kapansánan?** mah·dah·lee' bah ee·tohng poon·tah·hahn nahng mahy kah·pahn·sah·nahn

Sights

Where's…?	**Saán…?** sah·ahn…
– the battleground	**– ang pináglabánan** ahng pee·nahg·lah·bah·nahn
– the botanical garden	**– ang botánical gárden** ahng boh·tah·nee·kahl gahr·dehn
– the downtown area	**– ang báyan** ahng bah·yahn
– the fountain	**– ang fountain** ahng fahwn·tehyn
– the library	**– ang líbrary** ahng lahy·brah·ree
– the market	**– ang paléngke** ahng pah·lehng·keh
– the (war) memorial	**– ang libíngan (ng mgá bayáni)** ahng lee·bee·ngahn (nahng mah·ngah bah·yah·nee)
– the museum	**– ang muséo** ahng moo·seh·yoh
– the old town	**– ang lúmang báyan** ahng loo·mahng bah·yahn
– the opera house	**– ang ópera house** ahng oh·peh·rah hahws
– the palace	**– ang palásyo** ahng pah·lah·shoh
– the park	**– ang párke** ahng pahr·keh
– the shopping area	**– ang shópping área** ahng shah·peeng ehr·yah
– the theater	**– ang teátro** ahng teh·yaht·roh
– the town center	**– ang plása** ahng plah·sah
Can you show me on the map?	**Pwéde ba ninyóng iturò sa ákin sa mápa?** pweh·deh bah neen·yohng ee·too·roh' sah ah·keen sah mah·pah

▶ For directions, see page 36.

Of the many attractions in the Philippines, one must not miss the majestic Banaue Rice Terraces in Ifugao Province, north of Manila. The enthralling landscape formed by these rice fields was sculpted into the mountainsides by the Ifugao tribespeople 2000 years ago. For examples of breathtaking geological formations, schedule a trip to Mayon Volcano, with its near-perfect cone; Taal Volcano, one of the world's smallest volcanoes; and the underground river in St. Paul Subterranean Park, Palawan. Meanwhile, a visit to some of the well-preserved Spanish churches, such as Baclayon Church in Bohol, the Cathedral of St. Paul in Viban and Miagao Fortress Church in Iloilo, will give one a taste of Filipino history, culture and architecture combined. In Manila, Intramuros, the "walled city," also reveals features of Filipino life under Spanish rule. It is now a national monument and contains the Rizal Museum, with memorabilia of national hero Dr. Jose Rizal. Also in Manila is Malacañang Palace, office and residence of the Philippine president. It was built in the 18th century by a Spanish nobleman.

Impressions

It's…	…itó. …ee·<u>toh</u>
– amazing	– **Kahanga-hangà** kah·hah·ngah·<u>hah</u>·ngah'
– beautiful	– **Magandá** mah·gahn·<u>dah</u>
– boring	– **Nakákainíp** nah·<u>kah</u>·kah·ee·<u>neep</u>
– interesting	– **Interesánte** een·teh·reh·<u>sahn</u>·teh
– magnificent	– **Magnípiko** mahg·<u>nee</u>·pee·koh
– romantic	– **Romántiko** roh·<u>mahn</u>·tee·koh
– strange	– **Kakaibá** kah·kah·ee·<u>bah</u>
– stunning	– **Kagilá-gilalás** kah·gee·<u>lah</u>·gee·lah·<u>lahs</u>
– terrible	– **Teríble** teh·<u>reeb</u>·leh
– ugly	– **Pángit** <u>pah</u>·ngeet
I like it.	**Gustó ko itó.** goos·<u>toh</u> ko ee·<u>toh</u>
I don't like it.	**Hindî ko itó gustó.** heen·<u>dee</u>' koh ee·<u>toh</u> goos·<u>toh</u>

Religion

Where's…?	**Saán…?** sah·<u>ahn</u>…
– the cathedral	– **ang katedrál** ahng kah·tehd·<u>rahl</u>
– the *Catholic/ Protestant* church	– **ang simbáhang *Katóliko/Protestánte*** ahng seem·<u>bah</u>·hahng *kah·<u>toh</u>·lee·koh/ proh·tehs·<u>tahn</u>·teh*
– the mosque	– **ang móske** ahng <u>mohs</u>·keh
– the shrine	– **ang shrine** ahng shrahyn
– the synagogue	– **ang sýnagogue** ahng <u>see</u>·nah·gohg
– the temple	– **ang témplo** ahng <u>tehm</u>·ploh
What time is *mass/the service*?	**Anóng óras ang *mísa/serbísyo*?** ah·<u>nohng</u> <u>oh</u>·rahs ahng *<u>mee</u>·sah/sehr·<u>bee</u>·shoh*

Shopping

Essential

Where's the *market/ mall [shopping centre]*?	**Saán ang *paléngke/mall*?** sah·ahn ahng *pah·lehng·keh/mohl*
I'm just looking.	**Tumitingín lang akó.** too·mee·tee·ngeen lahng ah·koh
Can you help me?	**Pwéde ba ninyó akóng tulúngan?** pweh·deh bah neen·yoh ah·kohng·too·loo·ngahn
I'm being helped.	**May tumutúlong na sa ákin.** mahy too·moo·too·lohng nah sah ah·keen
How much?	**Magkáno?** mahg·kah·noh
That one, please.	**Iyóng isá, please.** ee·yohng ee·sah plees
That's all.	**Iyán lang.** ee·yahn lahng
Where can I pay?	**Saán akó pwédeng magbáyad?** sah·ahn ah·koh pweh·dehng mahg·bah·yahd
I'll pay *in cash/by credit card*.	**Magbabáyad akó ng *cash/crédit card*.** mahg·bah·bah·yahd ah·koh nahng *kahsh/ kreh·deet kahrd*
A receipt, please.	**Ang resíbo, please.** ahng reh·see·boh plees

Stores

Where's…?	**Saán…?** sah·ahn…
– the antiques store	**– ang tindáhan ng antík** ahng teen·dah·hahn nahng ahn·teek
– the bakery	**– ang panadérya** ahng pah·nah·dehr·yah
– the bookstore	**– ang bookstore** ahng book·stohr

Where's…?	**Saán…?** sah·<u>ahn</u>…
– the camera store	– **ang bilíhan ng kámera** ahng bee·<u>lee</u>·hahn nahng <u>kah</u>·meh·rah
– the clothing store	– **ang bilíhan ng damít** ahng bee·<u>lee</u>·hahn nahng dah·<u>meet</u>
– the delicatessen	– **ang délicatéssen** ahng <u>deh</u>·lee·kah·<u>teh</u>·sehn
– the department store	– **ang depártment store** ahng deh·<u>pahrt</u>·mehnt stohr
– the health food store	– **ang tindáhan ng mgá pagkáing pangkalusúgan** ahng teen·<u>dah</u>·hahn nahng mah·<u>ngah</u> pahg·<u>kah</u>·eehng pahng·kah·loo·<u>soo</u>·gahn

– the jeweler	– **ang tindáhan ng aláhas** ahng teen·<u>dah</u>·hahn nahng ah·<u>lah</u>·hahs
– the liquor store [off-licence]	– **ang tindáhan ng álak** ahng teen·<u>dah</u>·hahn nahng <u>ah</u>·lahk
– the market	– **ang paléngke** ahng pah·<u>lehng</u>·keh
– the music store	– **ang músic store** ahng <u>myoo</u>·seek stohr
– the pharmacy [chemist]	– **ang botíka** ahng boh·<u>tee</u>·kah
– the produce [grocery] store	– **ang grócery** ahng <u>groh</u>·seh·ree
– the shoe store	– **ang tindáhan ng sapátos** ahng teen·<u>dah</u>·hahn nahng sah·<u>pah</u>·tohs
– the shopping mall [shopping centre]	– **ang mall** ahng mohl
– the souvenir store	– **ang tindáhan ng mgá souvenír** ahng teen·<u>dah</u>·hahn nahng mah·<u>ngah</u> soh·vee·<u>neer</u>
– the supermarket	– **ang súpermárket** ahng <u>soo</u>·pehr·<u>mahr</u>·keht
– the tobacconist	– **ang nagtítindá ng tabáko** ahng nahg·<u>tee</u>·teen·dah nahng tah·<u>bah</u>·koh
– the toy store	– **ang tindáhan ng laruán** ahng teen·<u>dah</u>·hahn nahng lah·roo·<u>ahn</u>

Services

Can you recommend…?	**Pwéde ba kayóng magrékomendá…?** <u>pweh</u>·deh bah kah·<u>yohng</u> mahg·<u>reh</u>·koh·mehn·<u>dah</u>…
– a barber	– **ng barbéro** nahng bahr·<u>beh</u>·roh
– a dry cleaner	– **ng dry cléaner** nahng drahy <u>klee</u>·nehr
– a hairstylist	– **ng tagapag-áyos ng buhók** nahng tah·gah·pahg·<u>ah</u>·yohs nahng boo·<u>hohk</u>

Can you recommend…?	**Pwéde ba kayóng magrékomendá…?** pweh·deh bah kah·yohng mahg·reh·koh·mehn·dah…
– a laundromat [launderette]	**– ng palabáhan** nahng pah·lah·bah·hahn
– a nail salon	**– ng nail salón** nahng nehyl sah·lohn
– a spa	**– ng spa** nahng spah
– a travel agency	**– ng trável ágency** nahng trah·vehl ehy·jehn·see
Can you…this?	**Pwéde ba ninyóng…itó?** pweh·deh bah neen·yohng…ee·toh
– alter	**– bagúhin** bah·goo·heen
– clean	**– linísin** lee·nee·seen
– fix [mend]	**– ayúsin** ah·yoo·seen
– press	**– plantsahín** plahn·chah·heen
When will it be ready?	**Kailán itó pwédeng kúnin?** kah·ee·lahn ee·toh·pweh·dehng koo·neen

Spa

I'd like…	**Gustó kong…** goos·toh kohng…
– a bikini wax	**– magpa-bikíni wax** mahg·pah·bee·kee·nee wahx
– an eyebrow wax	**– magpa-wáx ng kílay** mahg·pah·wahx nahng kee·lahy
– a facial	**– magpa-fácial** mahg·pah·fehy·shahl
– a *manicure/ pedicure*	**– magpamánicure/magpapédicure** mahg·pah·mah·nee·kyoor/ mahg·pah·peh·dee·kyoor
– a massage	**– magpamasáhe** mahg·pah·mah·sah·heh

Do you *have/do*…?	**Méron ba kayóng…?** meh·rohn bah kah·<u>yohng</u>…
– acupuncture	**– acupúncture** ah·kyoo·<u>pahngk</u>·choor
– aromatherapy	**– arómathérapy** ah·<u>roh</u>·mah·<u>theh</u>·rah·pee
– oxygen treatment	**– óxygen treatment** <u>ohk</u>·see·jehn <u>treet</u>·mehnt
– a sauna	**– sauna** <u>sahw</u>·nah

Hair Salon

I'd like…	**Gustó kong…** goos·<u>toh</u> kohng…
– an appointment for *today/tomorrow*	**– magpa-appóintment** *ngayón/búkas* mahg·pah·ah·<u>pohynt</u>·mehnt *ngah·<u>yohn</u>/<u>boo</u>·kahs*
– my hair styled	**– magpaáyos ng áking buhók** mahg·pah·<u>ah</u>·yohs nahng <u>ah</u>·keeng boo·<u>hohk</u>
– a haircut	**– magpagupít** mahg·pah·goo·<u>peet</u>
– a trim	**– magpaiklî ng kontí** mahg·pah·eek·<u>lee</u>' nahng <u>kohn</u>·tee'
Not too short.	**Huwág masyádong maiklî.** hoo·<u>wahg</u> mah·<u>shah</u>·dohng mah·eek·<u>lee</u>'
Shorter here.	**Mas maiklî díto.** mahs mah·eek·<u>lee</u>' <u>dee</u>·toh

Sales Help

When do you *open/close*?	**Kailán kayó** *nagbubukás/nagsasará*? kah·ee·<u>lahn</u> kah·yoh *nahg·boo·boo·<u>kahs</u>/ nahg·sah·sah·<u>rah</u>*
Where's…?	**Saán…?** sah·<u>ahn</u>…
– the cashier	**– ang kahéra** ahng kah·<u>heh</u>·rah
– the escalator	**– ang éscalator** ahng <u>ehs</u>·kah·lehy·tohr
– the elevator [lift]	**– ang élevator** ahng <u>eh</u>·leh·behy·tohr
– the fitting room	**– ang fítting room** ahng <u>fee</u>·teeng room
– the store directory	**– ang direktóryo ng tindáhan** ahng dee·rehk·<u>tohr</u>·yoh nahng teen·<u>dah</u>·hahn

Can you help me?	**Pwéde ba ninyó akóng tulúngan?** pweh·deh bah neen·yoh ah·kohng too·loo·ngahn
I'm just looking.	**Tumitingín lang akó.** too·mee·tee·ngeen lahng ah·koh
I'm being helped.	**May tumutúlong na sa ákin.** mahy too·moo·too·lohng nah sah ah·keen
Do you have…?	**Méron ba kayóng…?** meh·rohn bah kah·yohng…
Can you show me…?	**Pwéde ba ninyóng iturò sa ákin ang…?** pweh·deh bah neen·yohng ee·too·roh' sah ah·keen ahng…
Can you *ship/wrap* it?	**Pwéde ba ninyó itóng *ipadalá/balútin*?** pweh·deh bah neen·yoh ee·tohng *ee·pah·dah·lah/ bah·loo·teen*
How much?	**Magkáno?** mahg·kah·noh
That's all.	**Iyán lang.** ee·yahn lahng

▶ For clothing items, see page 139.

▶ For food items, see page 90.

▶ For souvenirs, see page 134.

You May Hear…

Pwéde ko ba kayóng tulúngan? pweh·deh koh bah kah·yohng too·loo·ngahn	Can I help you?
Sandalî lámang. sahn·dah·lee' lah·mahng	One moment.
Anó ang gustó ninyó? ah·noh ahng goos·toh neen·yoh	What would you like?
Méron pa ba? meh·rohn pah bah	Anything else?

You May See...

BUKÁS/SARÁDO	open/closed
SARÁDO PÁRA SA PANANGHALÍAN	closed for lunch
FÍTTING ROOM	fitting room
CASHIÉR	cashier
CASH ÓNLY	cash only
CRÉDIT CARDS ACCÉPTED	credit cards accepted
BÚSINESS HOURS	business hours
PASUKÁN/LABÁSAN	entrance/exit

Preferences

I'd like something...   **Gustó ko...** goos·toh koh...

– cheap/expensive   **– ng *múra/mahál*** nahng *moo·rah/mah·hahl*

– larger/smaller   **– ng mas *malakí/maliít*** nahng mahs *mah·lah·kee/mah·lee·eet*

– nicer   **– ng mas magandá** nahng mahs mah·gahn·dah

– from this region   **– ng mulâ sa rehiyóng itó** nahng moo·lah' sah reh·hee·yohng ee·toh

Around...pesos.   **Mgá...píso ang halagá.** mah·ngah...pee·soh ahng hah·lah·gah

Is it real?   **Túnay ba itó?** too·nahy bah ee·toh

Can you show me *this/that*?   **Pwéde ba ninyóng ipakíta sa ákin *itó/iyán*?** pweh·deh bah neen·yohng ee·pah·kee·tah sah ah·keen *ee·toh/ee·yahn*

Decisions

That's not quite what I want.   **Médyo hindî iyán ang gustó ko.** meh·joh heen·dee' ee·yahn ahng goos·toh koh

No, I don't like it.	**Hindî ko gustó iyán.** heen·dee' koh goos·toh ee·yahn
It's too expensive.	**Masyádong mahál.** mah·shah·dohng mah·hahl
I have to think about it.	**Pag-iisípan ko múna.** pahg·ee·ee·see·pahn koh moo·nah
I'll take it.	**Kukúnin ko itó.** koo·koo·neen koh ee·toh

Bargaining

That's too much.	**Masyádong mahál namán iyán.** mah·shah·dohng mah·hahl nah·mahn ee·yahn
I'll give you...	**Bibigyán kitá ng...** bee·beeg·yahn kee·tah nahng...
I have only... pesos.	**Méron lang akóng...píso.** meh·ron lahng ah·kohng...pee·soh
Is that your best price?	**Tapát na ba ang présyo mong iyán?** tah·paht nah bah ahng preh·shoh mohng ee·yahn
Can you give me a discount?	**Pwéde ba ninyóng bigyán akó ng diskwénto?** pweh·deh bah neen·yohng beeg·yahn ah·koh nahng dees·kwehn·toh

▶ For numbers, see page 181.

Paying

How much?	**Magkáno?** mahg·kah·noh
I'll pay...	**Magbabáyad akó...** mahg·bah·bah·yahd ah·koh...
– in cash	**– ng cash** nahng kahsh
– by credit card	**– ng crédit card** nahng kreh·deet kahrd
– by traveler's check [cheque]	**– ng tráveler's check** nahng trah·veh·lehrs chehk

Can I use this... card?	**Pwéde ko bang gamítin itóng...card?** pweh·deh koh bahng gah·mee·teen ee·tohng...kahrd
– ATM	**– ATM** ehy·tee·ehm
– credit	**– crédit** kreh·deet
– debit	**– débit** deh·beet
– gift	**– gift** geeft
A receipt, please.	**Ang resíbo, please.** ahng reh·see·boh plees

When it comes to purchasing things in the Philippines, cash is certainly king. However, major credit cards are widely accepted, especially throughout Metro Manila and most other large cities. Debit cards have also become quite popular. Some businesses will tack on a surcharge for credit or debit card payments. You can never go wrong with cash, especially in the provinces. When traveling outside urban areas, it is a good idea to carry small bills and small change.

You May Hear...

Paáno kayó magbabáyad? pah·ah·noh kah·yoh mahg·bah·bah·yahd	How are you paying?
Hindî tinanggáp ang inyóng crédit card. heen·dee' tee·nahng·gahp ahng een·yohng kreh·deet kahrd	Your credit card has been declined.
ID, please. ahy·dee plees	ID, please.
Hindî kamí tumatanggáp ng crédit card. heen·dee' kah·mee too·mah·tahng·gahp nahng kreh·deet kahrd	We don't accept credit cards.
Cash lang, please. kahsh lahng plees	Cash only, please.

Complaints

I'd like…	**Gustó kong…** goos·<u>toh</u> kohng…
– to exchange this	**– pápalitán itó** pah·pah·lee·<u>tahn</u> ee·<u>toh</u>
– a refund	**– mag-refúnd** mahg·reh·<u>fahnd</u>
– to see to the manager	**– makaúsap ang mánager** mah·kah·<u>oo</u>·sahp ahng <u>mah</u>·neh·jehr

Souvenirs

bottle of wine	**bóte ng álak** <u>boh</u>·teh nahng <u>ah</u>·lahk
box of chocolates	**kahón ng tsokoláte** kah·<u>hohn</u> nahng choh·koh·<u>lah</u>·teh
doll	**manikà** mah·<u>nee</u>·kah'
cloth of Philippine silk	**júsi** <u>hoo</u>·see
cloth of pineapple silk	**télang gawâ sa pinyá** <u>teh</u>·lahng gah·<u>wah</u>' sah peen·<u>yah</u>
key ring	**lagáyan ng susì** lah·<u>gah</u>·yahn nahng <u>soo</u>·see'
mother-of-pearl lamp	**lámpara na gawâ sa cápiz** <u>lahm</u>·pah·rah nah gah·<u>wah</u>' sah <u>kah</u>·peez
postcard	**póstcard** <u>pohst</u>·kahrd
pottery	**bangá** bah·<u>ngah</u>
T-shirt	**T-shirt** <u>tee</u>·shehrt
toy	**laruán** lah·roo·<u>ahn</u>

The Philippines is a shopper's paradise, especially when it comes to handicrafts and souvenirs. Popular items include baskets, placemats, handbags, T-shirts, caps, mother-of-pearl lamps, jewelry, wood carvings, paintings, silver and brassware. The selection is simply amazing, and the only problem will be which souvenirs to choose.

Can I see *this/that*?	**Pwéde ko bang makíta *itó/iyón*?** pweh·deh koh bahng mah·kee·tah ee·toh/ee·yohn
It's in the *window/ display case.*	**Nása *bintanà/estánte* iyón.** nah·sah been·tah·nah'/ehs·tahn·teh ee·yohn
I'd like…	**Gustó ko…** goos·toh koh…
– a battery	**– ng bateryá** nahng bah·tehr·yah
– a bracelet	**– ng pulséras** nahng pool·seh·rahs
– a brooch	**– ng brótse** nahng broh·cheh
– a clock	**– ng orasán** nahng oh·rah·sahn
– earrings	**– ng híkaw** nahng hee·kahw
– a necklace	**– ng kwintás** nahng kween·tahs
– a ring	**– ng singsíng** nahng seeng·seeng
– a watch	**– ng reló** nahng reh·loh
– copper	**– ng tansô** nahng tahn·soh'
– crystal	**– ng kristál** nahng krees·tahl
– cut glass	**– ng cut glass** nahng kaht glahs
– diamonds	**– ng diyamánte** nahng dee·yah·mahn·teh
– enamel	**– ng enámel** nahng eh·nah·mehl
– *white/yellow* gold	**– ng *putî/diláw* na gintô** nahng poo·tee'/dee·lahw nah geen·toh'
– pearls	**– ng pérlas** nahng pehr·lahs
– pewter	**– ng péwter** nahng pyoo·tehr
– platinum	**– ng plátinúm** nahng plah·tee·noom
– sterling silver	**– ng stérling sílver** nahng stehr·leeng seel·vehr
Is this real?	**Túnay ba itó?** too·nahy bah ee·toh

Is there a certificate for it?	**May sertípiko ba itó?**
	mahy sehr·<u>tee</u>·pee·koh bah ee·<u>toh</u>
Can you engrave it?	**Pwéde ba ninyóng ukitan itó?** <u>pweh</u>·deh
	bah neen·<u>yohng</u> oo·<u>kee</u>·tahn ee·<u>toh</u>

i

The Philippines is known as "The Pearl of the Orient," and not just because of its stunning beauty. Pearls are perhaps the most popular and sought-after jewelry item the country has on offer. Make sure to visit Virra Mall in Greenhills, San Juan, Metro Manila. Stalls run mostly by Muslim traders carry pearls of every variety: fresh water, cultured and the famous South Sea black pearls. You can buy them loose or in fashionably crafted designs.

The Cebu area is a major hub for jewelry exported worldwide. Jewelry produced by tribes in the mountains or valleys is also quite stunning and popular. A good place to begin your search for locally made jewelry is at one of the big handicraft stores.

Antiques

How old is it?	**Gaáno na katandá itó?** gah·ah·noh nah kah·tahn·<u>dah</u> ee·<u>toh</u>
Do you have anything from the…period?	**Méron ba kayó ng mulâ pa noóng panahón ng…?** <u>meh</u>·rohn bah kah·<u>yoh</u> nahng moo·<u>lah</u>' pah noh·<u>ohng</u> pah·nah·<u>hohn</u> nahng…
Do I have to fill out any forms?	**May kailángan ba akóng sagután na form?** mahy kah·ee·<u>lah</u>·ngahn bah ah·<u>kohng</u> sah·goo·<u>tahn</u> nah fohrm
Is there a certificate of authenticity?	**May sertípiko ba ng pagíging awténtikó iyán?** mahy sehr·<u>tee</u>·pee·koh bah nahng pah·<u>gee</u>·geeng ahw·<u>tehn</u>·tee·<u>koh</u> ee·<u>yahn</u>

Clothing

I'd like…	**Gustó ko ng…** goos·<u>toh</u> koh nahng…
Can I try this on?	**Pwéde ko bang isúkat itó?** <u>pweh</u>·deh koh bahng ee·<u>soo</u>·kaht ee·<u>toh</u>
It doesn't fit.	**Hindî kásya.** heen·<u>dee</u>' <u>kah</u>·shah
It's too…	**Masyádong…** mah·<u>shah</u>·dohng…
– big/small	**– malakí/maliít** mah·lah·<u>kee</u>/mah·lee·<u>eet</u>
– short/long	**– maiklî/mahabà** mah·eek·<u>lee</u>'/mah·<u>hah</u>·bah'
– tight/loose	**– masikíp/maluwáng** mah·see·<u>keep</u>/ mah·loo·<u>wahng</u>
Do you have this in size…?	**May ganitó bang size…?** mahy gah·nee·<u>toh</u> bahng sahyz…
Do you have this in a *bigger/ smaller* size?	**Méron ba kayóng mas *malakí/maliít* na size nitó?** <u>meh</u>·rohn bah kah·<u>yohng</u> mahs *mah·lah·<u>kee</u>/mah·lee·<u>eet</u>* nah sahyz nee·<u>toh</u>

▶For numbers, see page 181.

Bágay iyán sa inyó. bah·gahy ee·<u>yahn</u> sah een·<u>yoh</u>	That looks great on you.
Kásya ba sa inyó? <u>kah</u>·shah bah sah een·<u>yoh</u>	How does it fit?
Walâ kamí ng size ninyó. wah·<u>lah</u>' kah·<u>mee</u> nahng sahyz neen·<u>yoh</u>	We don't have your size.

You May See…

PANLALÁKI	men's
PAMBABÁE	women's
PAMBATÀ	children's

Color

I'd like something…	**Gustó ko…** goos·<u>toh</u> koh…
– beige	**– ng beige** nahng behyj
– black	**– ng itím** nahng ee·<u>teem</u>
– blue	**– ng asúl** nahng ah·<u>sool</u>
– brown	**– ng brown** nahng brahwn
– green	**– ng bérde** nahng <u>behr</u>·deh
– gray	**– ng abó** nahng ah·<u>boh</u>
– orange	**– ng órange** nahng <u>oh</u>·rehynj
– pink	**– ng pink** nahng peengk
– purple	**– ng púrple** nahng <u>pohr</u>·pohl
– red	**– ng pulá** nahng poo·<u>lah</u>
– white	**– ng putî** nahng poo·<u>tee</u>'
– yellow	**– ng diláw** nahng dee·<u>lahw</u>

Clothes and Accessories

backpack	**báckpack**	bahk·pahk
belt	**sinturón**	seen·too·rohn
bikini	**bikíni**	bee·kee·nee
blouse	**blúsa**	bloo·sah
bra	**bra**	brah
briefs [underpants]	**brief**	breef
coat	**amerikána**	ah·meh·ree·kah·nah
dress	**bestída**	behs·tee·dah
hat	**sombréro**	sohm·breh·roh
jacket	**jácket**	jah·keht
jeans	**pantalóng maóng**	pahn·tah·lohng mah·ohng
pajamas [pyjamas]	**pajáma**	pah·jah·mah
pants [trousers]	**pantalón**	pahn·tah·lohn
pantyhose [tights]	**pántyhose**	pahn·tee·hohws
purse [handbag]	**bag**	bahg
raincoat	**kapóte**	kah·poh·teh
scarf	**bandána**	bahn·dah·nah
shorts	**shorts**	shohrts
skirt	**pálda**	pahl·dah
socks	**médyas**	meh·jahs
suit	**suit**	soot
sunglasses	**súnglasses**	sahn·glah·sehs
sweater	**swéater**	sweh·tehr
sweatshirt	**swéatshirt**	sweht·shert
swimsuit	**swimsuit**	sweem·soot
T-shirt	**T-shirt**	tee·shehrt

| tie | **kurbáta** koor·bah·tah |
| underwear | **únderwear** ahn·dehr·wehyr |

Fabric

I'd like…	**Gustó ko…** goos·toh koh…
– cotton	**– ng kóton** nahng koh·tohn
– denim	**– ng maóng** nahng mah·ohng
– lace	**– ng lace** nahng lehys
– leather	**– ng leather** nahng leh·ther
– linen	**– ng línen** nahng lee·nehn
– silk	**– ng séda** nahng seh·dah
– wool	**– ng lána** nahng lah·nah
Is it machine washable?	**Pwéde bang labahán itó sa wáshing machíne?** pweh·deh bahng lah·bah·han ee·toh sah wah·sheeng mah·sheen

Shoes

I'd like…	**Gustó ko…** goos·toh koh…
– high-heels/flats	**– ng *mataás ang/waláng* takóng** nahng *mah·tah·ahs ahng/wah·lahng* tah·kohng
– boots	**– ng bóta** nahng boh·tah
– flip-flops	**– ng tsinélas** nahng chee·neh·lahs
– hiking boots	**– ng bótang pang-híking** nahng boh·tahng pahng·hahy·keeng
– loafers	**– ng loafers** nahng lohw·fehrs
– sandals	**– ng sandályas** nahng sahn·dahl·yahs
– shoes	**– ng sapátos** nahng sah·pah·tohs
– slippers	**– ng tsinélas** nahng chee·neh·lahs
– sneakers	**– ng rúbber shoes** nahng rah·behr shoos

Sizes

Size…	**Size…** sahyz…
– extra small (XS)	**– éxtra small (XS)** <u>ehx</u>·trah smohl (ehx·ehs)
– small (S)	**– small (S)** smohl (ehs)
– medium (M)	**– médium (M)** <u>mee</u>·dee·yoom (ehm)
– large (L)	**– large (L)** lahrj (ehl)
– extra large (XL)	**– éxtra large (XL)** <u>ehx</u>·trah lahrj (ehx·ehl)
– plus	**– éxtra éxtra large (XXL)** <u>ehx</u>·trah <u>ehx</u>·trah lahrj (ehx·ehx·ehl)

Newsstand and Tobacconist ——————

Do you sell English-language newspapers?	**Nagbebénta ba kayó ng dyáryo sa Inglés?** nahg·beh·<u>behn</u>·tah bah kah·<u>yoh</u> nahng <u>jahr</u>·yoh sah eeng·<u>lehs</u>
I'd like…	**Gustó ko…** goos·<u>toh</u> koh…
– candy [sweets]	**– ng kéndi** nahng <u>kehn</u>·dee
– chewing gum	**– ng chéwing gum** nahng <u>choo</u>·weeng gahm
– a cigar	**– ng sigarílyo** nahng see·gah·<u>reel</u>·yoh
– a *pack/carton* of cigarettes	**– ng isáng *pakéte/kartón* ng sigarílyo** nahng ee·<u>sahng</u> *pah·<u>keh</u>·teh/kahr·<u>tohn</u>* nahng see·gah·<u>reel</u>·yoh
– a lighter	**– ng líghter** nahng <u>lahy</u>·tehr
– a magazine	**– ng mágasín** nahng <u>mah</u>·gah·<u>seen</u>
– matches	**– ng mgá pósporó** nahng mah·<u>ngah</u> pohs·poh·<u>roh</u>
– a newspaper	**– ng dyáryo** nahng <u>jahr</u>·yoh
– paper	**– ng papél** nahng pah·<u>pehl</u>
– a pen	**– ng bállpen** nahng <u>bohl</u>·pehn

I'd like…	**Gustó ko…** goos·<u>toh</u> koh…
– a postcard	**– ng póstcard** nahng <u>pohst</u>·kahrd
– a *road/town* map of…	**– ng mápa ng *daán/báyan* ng…** nahng <u>mah</u>·pah nahng *dah·<u>ahn</u>/<u>bah</u>·yahn* nahng…
– stamps	**– ng mgá sélyo** nahng mah·<u>ngah</u> <u>sehl</u>·yoh

There are several dozen daily newspapers produced in English, including Philippine Daily Inquirer, Philippine Star and Manila Bulletin. These can be bought from any of the newsstands and convenience store chains. Bookstores and hotels sell Asian versions of popular magazines like Time and Newsweek, as well as the International Herald Tribune, the Asian Wall Street Journal and the Financial Times. Philippine versions of popular, international magazines are widely distributed.

Photography

I'd like… camera.	**Gustó ko ng…kámera.** goos·<u>toh</u> koh nahng…<u>kah</u>·meh·rah
– an automatic	**– automátic na** ahw·toh·<u>mah</u>·teek nah
– a digital	**– dígital na** <u>dee</u>·jee·tahl nah
– a disposable	**– dispósable na** dees·<u>pohw</u>·sah·bohl nah
I'd like…	**Gustó ko…** goos·<u>toh</u> koh…
– a battery	**– ng bateryá** nahng bah·tehr·<u>yah</u>
– digital prints	**– ng dígital prints** nahng <u>dee</u>·jee·tahl preents
– a memory card	**– ng mémory card** nahng <u>meh</u>·moh·ree kahrd
Can I print digital photos here?	**Pwéde ba akóng mag-print ng dígital na mgá retráto díto?** <u>pweh</u>·deh bah ah·<u>kohng</u> mahg·<u>preent</u> nahng <u>dee</u>·jee·tahl nah mah·<u>ngah</u> reht·<u>rah</u>·toh <u>dee</u>·toh

Sports and Leisure

Essential

When's the game?	**Kailán ang larô?** kah·ee·<u>lahn</u> ahng lah·<u>roh</u>'
Where's…?	**Saán…?** sah·<u>ahn</u>…
– the beach	**– ang beach** ahng beech
– the park	**– ang párke** ahng <u>pahr</u>·keh
– the pool	**– ang pool** ahng pool
Is it safe to swim here?	**Ligtás bang lumangóy díto?** leeg·<u>tahs</u> bahng loo·mah·<u>ngohy</u> dee·toh
Can I rent [hire] golf clubs?	**Pwéde ba akóng magrénta ng mgá golf club?** <u>pweh</u>·deh bah ah·<u>kohng</u> mahg·<u>rehn</u>·tah nahng mah·<u>ngah</u> gohlf klahb
How much per hour?	**Magkáno báwat óras?** mahg·<u>kah</u>·noh <u>bah</u>·waht <u>oh</u>·rahs
How far is it to…?	**Gaáno kalayò itó sa…?** gah·<u>ah</u>·noh kah·<u>lah</u>·yoh' ee·<u>toh</u> sah…
Show me on the map, please.	**Pakiturò mo sa ákin sa mápa, please.** pah·kee·<u>too</u>·roh' moh sah <u>ah</u>·keen sah <u>mah</u>·pah plees

Spectator Sports

When's… game/match?	**Kailán ang *larô/lában*…?** kah·ee·<u>lahn</u> ahng *lah·<u>roh</u>'/<u>lah</u>·bahn*…
– the baseball	**– sa béysbol** sah <u>behys</u>·bohl
– the basketball	**– sa básketból** sah <u>bahs</u>·keht·<u>bohl</u>
– the boxing	**– sa bóksing** sah <u>bohk</u>·seeng
– the golf	**– sa golf** sah gohlf

When's... game/match?	**Kailán ang *larô/lában*...?** kah·ee·<u>lahn</u> ahng *lah·<u>roh</u>'/<u>lah</u>·bahn*...
– the (ice) hockey	**– sa (ice) hóckey** sah (ahys) <u>hah</u>·kehy
– the rugby	**– sa rúgby** sah <u>rahg</u>·bee
– the soccer [football]	**– sa sóccer** sah <u>sah</u>·kehr
– the tennis	**– sa ténnis** sah <u>teh</u>·nees
– the volleyball	**– sa vólleyból** sah <u>vah</u>·lee·<u>bohl</u>
Who's playing?	**Síno ang maglalarô?** <u>see</u>·noh ahng mahg·lah·lah·<u>roh</u>'
Where's the racetrack/stadium?	**Saán ang *kareráhan/stádium*** sah·<u>ahn</u> ahng kah·reh·<u>rah</u>·hahn/ees·<u>tehyd</u>·yoom
Where can I place a bet?	**Saán akó pwédeng pumustá?** sah·<u>ahn</u> ah·<u>koh</u> <u>pweh</u>·dehng poo·moos·<u>tah</u>

▶ For ticketing, see page 20.

Participating

Where *is/are*...?	**Saán...?** sah·<u>ahn</u>...
– the golf course	**– ang golf course** ahng gohlf kohrs
– the gym	**– ang gym** ahng jeem
– the park	**– ang párke** ahng <u>pahr</u>·keh
– the tennis courts	**– ang ténnis courts** ahng <u>teh</u>·nees kohrts
How much per...?	**Magkáno báwat...?** mahg·<u>kah</u>·noh <u>bah</u>·waht...
– day	**– áraw** <u>ah</u>·rahw
– hour	**– óras** <u>oh</u>·rahs
– game	**– larô** lah·<u>roh</u>'
– round	**– round** rahwnd

i

While the rest of Asia goes bonkers over soccer, Filipinos simply adore basketball. Hoops and courts of varying styles can be found literally everywhere throughout the country. Philippine Basketball Association (PBA) games appear on TV year-round, as do semi-pro and college games. Filipinos also love billiards and pool, and the country produces the world's best players. Boxing also has a long and proud tradition in the Philippines. Another favorite sport is cockfighting, which is perfectly legal. The raucous crowds all wagering on their favorite roosters make for one of the Philippines' most colorful sporting scenes.

Can I rent [hire]...?	**Pwéde ba akóng magrénta...?** pweh·deh bah ah·<u>kohng</u> mahg·<u>rehn</u>·tah...
– golf clubs	**– ng mgá club** nahng mah·<u>ngah</u> klahb
– equipment	**– ng gámit** nahng <u>gah</u>·meet
– a racket	**– ng rakéta** nahng rah·<u>keh</u>·tah

At the Beach/Pool

Where's the *beach/pool*?	**Saán ang *beach/pool*?** sah·<u>ahn</u> ahng *beech/pool*
Is there...?	**Méron bang...?** <u>meh</u>·rohn bahng...
– a kiddie [paddling] pool	**– pool na pambatà** pool nah pahm·<u>bah</u>·tah'
– an *indoor/outdoor* pool	**– nása *loób/labás* na pool** <u>nah</u>·sah *loo·<u>ohb</u>/lah·<u>bahs</u>* nah pool
– a lifeguard	**– lífeguard** <u>lahyf</u>·gahrd
Is it safe...?	**Ligtás ba itó...?** leeg·<u>tahs</u> bah ee·<u>toh</u>...
– to swim	**– na languyán** nah lah·ngoo·<u>yahn</u>
– to dive	**– na sisíran** nah see·<u>see</u>·rahn
– for children	**– pára sa mgá batà** <u>pah</u>·rah sah mah·<u>ngah</u> <u>bah</u>·tah'

I'd like to rent [hire]…	**Gustó kong magrénta…** goos·toh kohng mahg·rehn·tah…
– a deck chair	**– ng deck chair** nahng dehk chehyr
– diving equipment	**– ng gámit sa pagsísid** nahng gah·meet sah pahg·see·seed
– a jet ski	**– ng jet ski** nahng jeht skee
– a motorboat	**– ng bangkáng de motór** nahng bahng·kahng deh moh·tohr
– a rowboat	**– ng bangká** nahng bahng·kah
– snorkeling equipment	**– ng gámit sa snórkeling** nahng gah·meet sah snohr·kleeng
– a surfboard	**– ng súrfboard** nahng sehrf·bohrd
– an umbrella	**– ng páyong** nahng pah·yohng
– water skis	**– ng wáter skis** nahng wah·tehr skees
– a windsurfer	**– ng wíndsurfer** nahng weend·sehr·fehr
For…hours.	**Pára…óras.** pah·rah…oh·rahs

A tropical country with 7,107 islands can only mean one thing: endless stretches of white and golden sand beaches. The Philippines is known worldwide for its beautiful beaches. The most famous beach is on the tourist haven of Boracay Island. The cottony-soft beach of Boracay elicits wows from even the most jaded beachgoer. Other popular beach areas include Palawan, Puerto Galera, Batangas, San Fernando, La Union, Pagudpud, Cebu, Camiguin, Hundred Islands and Subic Bay. But these are just a small sampling. There are literally thousands of beaches, many virtually unexplored, waiting to be discovered. Remember, however, that Philippine beaches don't have lifeguards, so take extra precaution and ask the locals about the power of the currents and waves.

With bountiful beaches and mountains, and a year-round tropical climate, the Philippines is a haven for water sports. Some good surfing spots include Siargao Island in Mindanao, La Union in Northern Luzon and Catanduanes in the Bicol region. There are dozens of world-class scuba-diving spots, including the Tubbataha and Apo Reefs, and Puerto Galera in Mindoro. Snorkeling is widely accessible off most beaches. Rivers in the Cordillera mountain region have become popular places for canoeing, kayaking and white-water rafting. Windsurfing is popular in Batangas, Puerto Galera and Boracay. The close proximity of many islands makes for smooth sailboating. Boats with captains are easy to hire and make for a great way to see the islands.

In the Countryside

A map of…, please.	**Mápa…, please.** mah·pah…plees
– this region	**– ng rehiyóng itó** nahng reh·hee·yohng ee·toh
– the walking routes	**– ng rúta sa paglalakád** nahng roo·tah sah pahg·lah·lah·kahd
– the bike routes	**– ng rúta sa pagbibisikléta** nahng roo·tah sah pahg·bee·bee·seek·leh·tah
– the trails	**– ng mgá daánan** nahng mah·ngah dah·ah·nahn
Is it…?	**Itó ba ay…?** ee·toh bah ahy…
– easy	**– madalî** mah·dah·lee'
– difficult	**– mahírap** mah·hee·rahp
– far	**– malayò** mah·lah·yoh'
– steep	**– matarík** mah·tah·reek
I'm exhausted.	**Pagód na akó.** pah·gohd nah ah·koh
How far is it to…?	**Gaáno pa kalayò sa…?** gah·ah·noh pah kah·lah·yoh' sah…

Show me on the map, please.	**Pakiturò mo sa ákin sa mápa, please.** pah·kee·<u>too</u>·roh' moh sah <u>ah</u>·keen sah <u>mah</u>·pah plees
I'm lost.	**Nawawalâ akó.** nah·wah·wah·<u>lah</u>' ah·<u>koh</u>
Where's...?	**Saán...?** sah·<u>ahn</u>...
– the bridge	**– ang tuláy** ahng too·<u>lahy</u>
– the cave	**– ang kuwéba** ahng koo·<u>weh</u>·bah
– the cliff	**– ang bangín** ahng bah·<u>ngeen</u>
– the farm	**– ang búkid** ahng <u>boo</u>·keed
– the field	**– ang párang** ahng <u>pah</u>·rahng
– the forest	**– ang gúbat** ahng <u>goo</u>·baht
– the hill	**– ang buról** ahng boo·<u>rohl</u>
– the lake	**– ang lawà** ahng <u>lah</u>·wah'
– the mountain	**– ang bundók** ahng boon·<u>dohk</u>
– the nature preserve	**– ang protektádong kalikásan** ahng proh·tehk·<u>tah</u>·dohng kah·lee·<u>kah</u>·sahn
– the overlook [viewpoint]	**– ang lugár na overlooking** ahng loo·<u>gahr</u> nah oh·vehr·<u>loo</u>·keeng
– the park	**– ang párke** ahng <u>pahr</u>·keh
– the path	**– ang daánan** ahng dah·<u>ah</u>·nahn
– the peak	**– ang tuktók** ahng took·<u>tohk</u>
– the picnic area	**– ang lugár na pwédeng magpíknik** ahng loo·<u>gahr</u> nah <u>pweh</u>·dehng mahg·<u>peek</u>·neek
– the pond	**– ang pond** ahng pahnd
– the rainforest	**– ang rainfórest** ahng rehyn·<u>foh</u>·rehst
– the river	**– ang ílog** ahng <u>ee</u>·lohg
– the sea	**– ang dágat** ahng <u>dah</u>·gaht
– the (thermal) spring	**– ang (hot) spring** ahng (haht) spreeng
– the stream	**– ang bátis** ahng <u>bah</u>·tees
– the valley	**– ang lambák** ahng lahm·<u>bahk</u>
– the waterfall	**– ang talón** ahng tah·<u>lohn</u>

Culture and Nightlife

Essential

What's there to do at night?	**Anó ang pwédeng gawín sa gabí?** ah·<u>noh</u> ahng pweh·dehng gah·ween sah gah·<u>bee</u>
Do you have a program of events?	**Méron ba kayóng listáhan ng mgá prográma?** <u>meh</u>·rohn bah kah·<u>yohng</u> lees·<u>tah</u>·hahn nahng mah·<u>ngah</u> prohg·<u>rah</u>·mah
What's playing tonight?	**Anó ang palabás ngayóng gabí?** ah·<u>noh</u> ahng pah·lah·<u>bahs</u> ngah·<u>yohng</u> gah·<u>bee</u>
Where's…?	**Saán…?** sah·<u>ahn</u>…
– the downtown area	**– ang plása** ahng <u>plah</u>·sah
– the bar	**– ang bar** ahng bahr
– the dance club	**– ang dance club** ahng dahns klahb
Is there a cover charge?	**Méron bang sérvice charge?** <u>meh</u>·rohn bahng <u>sehr</u>·vees· chahrj

Entertainment

Can you recommend…?	**Pwéde ba kayóng magrékomendá…?** <u>pweh</u>·deh bah kah·<u>yohng</u> mahg·<u>reh</u>·koh·mehn·<u>dah</u>…
– a ballet	**– ng ballét** nahng bah·<u>lehy</u>
– a concert	**– ng cóncert** nahng <u>kohn</u>·sehrt
– a movie	**– ng pelíkulá** nahng peh·<u>lee</u>·koo·lah
– an opera	**– ng ópera** nahng <u>oh</u>·peh·rah
– a play	**– ng dulâ** nahng doo·<u>lah'</u>
When does it *start/end*?	**Kailán itó *magsisimulâ/matatápos*?** kah·ee·<u>lahn</u> ee·toh *mahg·see·see·moo·<u>lah'</u>/ mah·tah·<u>tah</u>·pohs*

Where's…?	Saán…? sah·ahn…
– the concert hall	– ang cóncert hall ahng <u>kohn</u>·sehrt hohl
– the opera house	– ang ópera house ahng <u>oh</u>·peh·rah hahws
– the theater	– ang sinehán ahng see·neh·<u>hahn</u>
What's the dress code?	Anó ang dress code? ah·<u>noh</u> ahng drehs kohwd
I like…	Gustó ko… goos·<u>toh</u> koh…
– classical music	– ng clássical músic nahng <u>klah</u>·see·kahl <u>myoo</u>·seek
– folk music	– ng folk músic nahng fohk <u>myoo</u>·seek
– jazz	– ng jazz nahng jahz
– pop music	– ng pop músic nahng pahp <u>myoo</u>·seek
– rap	– ng rap nahng rahp

▶ For ticketing, see page 20.

 The Philippines is a nation of colorful **fiestas** (festivals) and celebrations happening year-round. Some of the major events include the Sinulog Festival in Cebu; the Ati-Atihan Festival in Kalibo, Aklan; the Dinagyang Festival in Iloilo and the Panagbenga Festival in Baguio City. Check the major daily newspapers for information.

You May Hear…

Sold out na. sohld ahwt nah	We're sold out.
Cash o crédit? kahsh oh <u>kreh</u>·deet	Cash or credit?
Patayín ang inyóng mgá cell phone, please. pah·tah·<u>yeen</u> ahng een·<u>yohng</u> mah·<u>ngah</u> sehl fohwn plees	Turn off your cell [mobile] phones, please.

Nightlife

What's there to do at night?	**Anó ang pwédeng gawín sa gabí?** ah·<u>noh</u> ahng pweh·dehng gah·<u>ween</u> sah gah·<u>bee</u>
Can you recommend…?	**Pwéde ba kayóng magrékomendá…?** <u>pweh</u>·deh bah kah·<u>yohng</u> mahg·<u>reh</u>·koh·mehn·dah…
– a bar	**– ng bar** nahng bahr
– a casino	**– ng casíno** nahng kah·<u>see</u>·noh
– a dance club	**– ng dance club** nahng dahns klahb
– a gay club	**– ng gay club** nahng gehy klahb
– a jazz club	**– ng jazz club** nahng jahz klahb
– a club with Filipino music	**– ng club na may músikang Filipíno** nahng klahb nah mahy <u>moo</u>·see·kahng fee·lee·<u>pee</u>·noh
Is there live music?	**Méron bang tumutugtóg ng live?** <u>meh</u>·rohn bahng too·moo·toog·<u>tohg</u> nahng lahyv
How do I get there?	**Paáno akó makákapuntá doón?** pah·<u>ah</u>·noh ah·<u>koh</u> mah·<u>kah</u>·kah·poon·<u>tah</u> doo·<u>ohn</u>
Is there a cover charge?	**Méron bang sérvice charge?** <u>meh</u>·rohn bahng <u>sehr</u>·vees chahrj
Let's go dancing.	**Sayáw táyo.** sah·<u>yahw</u> tah·yoh

▼ *Special Needs*

Business Travel

Essential

I'm here on business.	**Nandíto akó pára sa offícial búsiness.** nahn-<u>dee</u>-toh ah-<u>koh</u> <u>pah</u>-rah sah oh-<u>fee</u>-shahl <u>bees</u>-nehs
Here's my business card.	**Etó ang áking búsiness card.** eh-<u>toh</u> ahng <u>ah</u>-keeng <u>bees</u>-nehs kahrd
Can I have your card?	**Pwéde bang makahingî ng inyóng búsiness card?** <u>pweh</u>-deh bahng mah-kah-hee-<u>ngee</u>' nahng een-<u>yohng</u> <u>bees</u>-nehs kahrd
I have a meeting with…	**May meeting akó kay…** mahy <u>mee</u>-teeng ah-<u>koh</u> kahy…
Where's…?	**Saán…?** sah-<u>ahn</u>…
– the business center	**– ang búsiness cénter** ahng <u>bees</u>-nehs <u>sehn</u>-tehr
– the convention hall	**– ang convéntion hall** ahng kohn-<u>vehn</u>-shohn hohl
– the meeting room	**– ang meeting room** ahng <u>mee</u>-teeng room

A handshake is a common business greeting for both men and women. English is widely used in government and business sectors and, so, English greetings may be used. It is important to show respect for elders, professionals and persons holding key posts in government or business. Address these people by their titles, e.g., "Attorney Cruz," "Doctor Lopez," or simply as "sir" or "ma'am," unless the person prefers to be called by his or her first name. Business cards should be presented after introductions. Cultural mistakes include pointing directly at someone with your finger and staring or yelling at someone in public or in front of co-workers.

Business Communication

I'm here…	**Nandíto akó…** nahn·dee·toh ah·koh…
– on business	**– pára sa offícial búsiness** pah·rah sah oh·fee·shahl bees·nehs
– for a seminar	**– pára sa isáng seminár** pah·rah sah ee·sahng seh·mee·nahr
– for a conference	**– pára sa isáng kúmperensiyá** pah·rah sah ee·sahng koom·peh·rehn·see·yah
– for a meeting	**– pára sa isáng meeting** pah·rah sah ee·sahng mee·teeng
My name is…	**…ang pangálan ko.** …ahng pah·ngah·lahn koh
I have *a meeting/an appointment* with…	**May *meeting/appóintment* akó kay…** mahy *mee·teeng/ah·pohynt·mehnt* ah·koh kahy…
I need an interpreter.	**Kailángan ko ng intérpretér.** kah·ee·lah·ngahn koh nahng een·tehr·preh·tehr

I need to…	**Kailángan kong…** kah·ee·<u>lah</u>·ngahn kohng…
– make a call	**– tumáwag** too·<u>mah</u>·wahg
– make a photocopy	**– magpakópya** mahg·pah·<u>kohp</u>·yah
– send an e-mail	**– mag-émail** mahg·<u>ee</u>·mehyl
– send a fax	**– mag-fax** mahg·fahx
– send a package (overnight)	**– magpadalá ng páckage (overnight)** mahg·pah·dah·<u>lah</u> nahng <u>pah</u>·kehyj (oh·vehr·nahyt)
It was a pleasure to meet you.	**Isáng kasiyáhang makilála ka.** ee·<u>sahng</u> kah·see·<u>yah</u>·hahng mah·kee·<u>lah</u>·lah kah

▶ For internet and communications, see page 53.

You May Hear…

Méron ba kayóng appóintment? <u>meh</u>·rohn bah kah·<u>yohng</u> ah·<u>pohynt</u>·mehnt	Do you have an appointment?
Kaníno? kah·<u>nee</u>·noh	With whom?
Nása meeting siyá. <u>nah</u>·sah <u>mee</u>·teeng see·<u>yah</u>	He/She is in a meeting.
Sandalî lang, please. sahn·dah·<u>lee</u>' lahng plees	One moment, please.
Maupô kayó. mah·oo·<u>poh</u>' kah·<u>yoh</u>	Have a seat.
Salámat sa inyóng pagdaló. sah·<u>lah</u>·maht sah een·<u>yohng</u> pahg·dah·<u>loh</u>	Thank you for coming.

Travel with Children

Essential

Is there a discount for kids?	**May diskwéntó ba pára sa mgá batà?** mahy dees-kwehn-toh bah pah-rah sah mah-ngah bah-tah'
Can you recommend a babysitter?	**Pwéde ba kayóng magrékomendá ng taga-alága ng batà?** pweh-deh bah kah-yohng mahg-reh-koh-mehn-dah nahng tah-gah-ah-lah-gah nahng bah-tah'
Do you have a *child's seat/highchair*?	**Méron ba kayóng *upuán ng batà/highchair*?** meh-rohn bah kah-yohng oo-poo-ahn nahng bah-tah'/hahy-chehyr
Where can I change the baby?	**Saán ko pwédeng palitán ang báby?** sah-ahn koh pweh-dehng pah-lee-tahn ahng behy-bee

Fun with Kids

Can you recommend something for kids?	**Pwéde ba kayóng magrékomendá ng káhit na anó pára sa mgá batà?** pweh-deh bah kah-yohng mahg-reh-koh-mehn-dah nahng kah-heet nah ah-noh pah-rah sah mah-ngah bah-tah'
Where's…?	**Saán…?** sah-ahn…
– the amusement park	– **ang amúsement park** ahng ah-myoos-mehnt pahrk
– the arcade	– **ang arcáde** ahng ahr-kehyd
– the kiddie [paddling] pool	– **ang pool na pambatà** ahng pool nah pahm-bah-tah'
– the park	– **ang párke** ahng pahr-keh
– the playground	– **ang pláyground** ahng plehy-grahwnd
– the zoo	– **ang zoo** ahng zoo

Are kids allowed?	**Pwéde ba ang mgá batà?** <u>pweh</u>·deh bah ahng mah·<u>ngah</u> <u>bah</u>·tah'
Is it safe for kids?	**Ligtás ba itó pára sa mgá batà?** leeg·<u>tahs</u> bah ee·<u>toh</u> <u>pah</u>·rah sah mah·<u>ngah</u> <u>bah</u>·tah'
Is it suitable for… -year-olds?	**Bágay ba itó sa mgá…taóng gúlang?** <u>bah</u>·gahy bah ee·<u>toh</u> sah mah·<u>ngah</u>…tah·ohng goo·lahng

▶ For numbers, see page 181.

You May Hear…

Ang cute namán! ahng kyoot nah·<u>mahn</u>	How cute!
Anó ang pangálan niyá? ah·<u>noh</u> ahng pah·<u>ngah</u>·lahn nee·<u>yah</u>	What's his/her name?
Iláng taón na siyá? ee·<u>lahng</u> tah·<u>ohn</u> nah see·<u>yah</u>	How old is he/she?

Basic Needs for Kids

Do you have…?	**Méron ba kayóng…?** meh·rohn bah kah·yohng…
– a baby bottle	– **bóte ng batà** boh·teh nahng bah·tah'
– baby food	– **pagkáin ng batà** pahg·kah·een nahng bah·tah'
– baby wipes	– **báby wipes** behy·bee wahyps
– a car seat	– **car seat** kahr seet
– a children's menu/portion	– **menú/sérving pára sa mgá batà** mee·noo/sehr·veeng pah·rah sah mah·ngah bah·tah'

▶ For dining with kids, see page 69.

– a child's seat/ highchair	– **upúan ng batà/high chair** oo·poo·ahn nahng bah·tah'/hahy·chehyr
– a crib/cot	– **krib/tehéras** kreeb/tee·heh·rahs
– diapers [nappies]	– **mgá lampín** mah·ngah lahm·peen
– formula [baby food]	– **báby food** behy·bee food
– a pacifier [soother]	– **pacifíer** pah·see·fah·yehr
– a playpen	– **pláypen** plehy·pehn
– a stroller [pushchair]	– **stróller** ees·troh·lehr
Where can I breastfeed/change the baby?	**Saán akó pwédeng magpasúso/magpalít ng báby?** sah·ahn ah·koh pweh·dehng mahg·pah·soo·soh/mahg·pah·leet nahng behy·bee

Babysitting

Can you recommend a babysitter?	**Pwéde ba kayóng magrékomendá ng taga-alága ng batà?** pweh·deh bah kah·yohng mahg·reh·koh·mehn·dah nahng tah·gah·ah·lah·gah nahng bah·tah'
What's the charge?	**Magkáno ang báyad?** mahg·kah·noh ahng bah·yahd

| I'll be back by… | **Babalík akó nang…** bah·bah·<u>leek</u> ah·<u>koh</u> nahng… |
| I can be reached at… | **Pwéde akóng tawágan sa…** <u>pweh</u>·deh ah·<u>kohng</u> tah·<u>wah</u>·gahn sah… |

▶ For time, see page 183.

▶ For numbers, see page 181.

Health and Emergency

Can you recommend a pediatrician?	**Pwéde ba kayóng magrékomendá ng pediatrícian?** <u>pweh</u>·deh bah kah·<u>yohng</u> mahg·<u>reh</u>·koh·mehn·<u>dah</u> nahng pehd·yah·<u>tree</u>·shahn
My child is allergic to…	**May állergy ang anák ko sa…** mahy <u>ah</u>·lehr·jee ahng ah·<u>nahk</u> koh sah…
My child is missing.	**Nawáwalâ ang anák ko.** nah·<u>wah</u>·wah·<u>lah</u>' ahng ah·<u>nahk</u> koh
Have you seen a *boy/girl*?	**Nakakíta ba kayó ng bátang *laláki/babáe*?** nah·kah·<u>kee</u>·tah bah kah·<u>yoh</u> nahng <u>bah</u>·tahng *lah·<u>lah</u>·kee/bah·<u>bah</u>·eh*

▶ For food items, see page 90.

▶ For health, see page 166.

▶ For police, see page 163.

Essential

Is there…?	**Méron bang…?** <u>meh</u>·rohn bahng…
– access for the disabled	**– daánan pára sa may kapansánan** dah·<u>ah</u>·nahn <u>pah</u>·rah sah mahy kah·pahn·<u>sah</u>·nahn
– a wheelchair ramp	**– rámpa pára sa wheelchair** <u>rahm</u>·pah <u>pah</u>·rah sah <u>weel</u>·chehyr
– a handicapped-[disabled-] accessible toilet	**– CR pára sa may kapansánan** see·ahr <u>pah</u>·rah sah mahy kah·pahn·<u>sah</u>·nahn
I need…	**Kailángan ko…** kah·ee·<u>lah</u>·ngahn koh…
– assistance	**– ng túlong** nahng <u>too</u>·lohng
– an elevator [a lift]	**– ng elevátor** nahng eh·leh·<u>vehy</u>·tohr
– a ground-floor room	**– ng kuwárto sa ground floor** <u>nahng</u> koo·<u>wahr</u>·toh sah <u>grahwnd</u> flohr

Getting Help

I'm…	**Akó ay…** ah·<u>koh</u> ahy…
– disabled	**– may kapansánan** mahy kah·pahn·<u>sah</u>·nahn
– visually impaired	**– bulág** boo·<u>lahg</u>
– hearing impaired/ deaf	**– bingí** bee·<u>ngee</u>
– unable to *walk far/use the stairs*	**– hindî *makalákad ng maláyo/ makagámit ng hagdán*** heen·<u>dee</u>' mah·kah·<u>lah</u>·kahd nahng mah·<u>lah</u>·yoh/ mah·kah·<u>gah</u>·meet nahng hahg·<u>dahn</u>

Please speak louder.	**Pakílakás lang ang pagsasalitâ.**
	pah·*kee*·lah·*kahs* lahng ahng pahg·sah·sah·lee·*tah'*
Can I bring my wheelchair?	**Pwéde ko bang dalhín ang wheelchair ko?** *pweh*·deh koh bahng dahl·*heen* ahng *weel*·chehyr koh
Are guide dogs permitted?	**Pinapayágan ba ang mgá guide dog?** pee·nah·pah·*yah*·gahn bah ahng mah·*ngah* gahyd dohg
Can you help me?	**Pwéde ba ninyó akóng tulúngan?** *pweh*·deh bah neen·*yoh* ah·*kohng* too·*loo*·ngahn
Please *open/hold* the door.	***Pakíbuksán/Pakíhawákan* ang pintúan.** *pah·kee·book·sahn/pah·kee·hah·wah·kahn* ahng peen·*too*·ahn

▼ Resources

Emergencies

Essential

Help!	**Saklólo!** sahk·<u>loh</u>·loh
Go away!	**Alís!** ah·<u>lees</u>
Stop, thief!	**Tígil, magnanákaw!** <u>tee</u>·geel mahg·nah·<u>nah</u>·kahw
Get a doctor!	**Tumáwag kayó ng doktór!** too·<u>mah</u>·wahg kah·<u>yoh</u> nahng dohk·<u>tohr</u>
Fire!	**Sunóg!** soo·<u>nohg</u>
I'm lost.	**Nawawalâ akó.** nah·wah·wah·<u>lah</u>' ah·<u>koh</u>
Can you help me?	**Pwéde bang tulúngan ninyó akó?** <u>pweh</u>·deh bahng too·<u>loo</u>·ngahn neen·<u>yoh</u> ah·<u>koh</u>

Police

Essential

Call the police!	**Tumáwag kayó ng pulís!** too·<u>mah</u>·wahg kah·<u>yoh</u> nahng poo·<u>lees</u>
Where's the police station?	**Saán ang estasyón ng pulís?** sah·<u>ahn</u> ahng ehs·tah·<u>shohn</u> nahng poo·<u>lees</u>
There was an *accident/attack*.	**Mérong *aksidénte/pag-atáke*.** <u>meh</u>·rong *ahk·see·<u>dehn</u>·teh/pahg·ah·<u>tah</u>·keh*
My child is missing.	**Nawawalâ ang anák ko.** nah·wah·wah·<u>lah</u>' ahng ah·<u>nahk</u> koh

I need…	**Kailángan ko…** kah·ee·<u>lah</u>·ngahn koh…
– an interpreter	**– ng isáng intérpreter** nahng ee·<u>sahng</u> een·<u>tehr</u>·preh·tehr
– to contact my lawyer	**– na kóntakin ang áking abogádo** nah <u>kohn</u>·tah·keen ahng ah·keeng ah·boh·<u>gah</u>·doh
– to make a phone call	**– na tumáwag sa teléponó** nah too·<u>mah</u>·wahg sah teh·<u>leh</u>·poh·<u>noh</u>
– to contact the *embassy/consulate*	**– na kóntakin ang *émbaháda/konsuládo*** nah <u>kohn</u>·tah·keen ahng *ehm·bah·<u>hah</u>·dah/ kohn·soo·<u>lah</u>·doh*
I'm innocent.	**Inosénte akó.** ee·noh·<u>sehn</u>·teh ah·<u>koh</u>

You May Hear…

Sagután ang form na itó. sah·goo·<u>tahn</u> ahng fohrm nah ee·<u>toh</u>	Fill out this form.
Ang ID ninyó, please. ahng ahy·dee neen·<u>yoh</u> plees	Your identification, please.
***Kailán/Saán* itó nangyári?** kah·ee·<u>lahn</u>/ sah·<u>ahn</u> ee·<u>toh</u> nahng·<u>yah</u>·ree	*When/Where* did it happen?
Anó ang kanyáng itsúra? ah·<u>noh</u> ahng kahn·<u>yahng</u> eet·<u>soo</u>·rah	What does he/she look like?

 A few simple steps can save you a lot of hassle, especially if you have an emergency. Before arriving in the country, get the local number of your embassy and your airline. For additional phone numbers, dial 187 for directory assistance in Manila, or check the yellow or white pages. Dial 167 for emergency police assistance.

Lost Property and Theft

I'd like to report…	**Gustó kong i-repórt…** goos·<u>toh</u> kohng ee·reh·<u>pohrt</u>…
– a mugging	**– ang isáng pambubugbóg at pagnanákaw** ahng ee·<u>sahng</u> pahm·boo·boog·<u>bohg</u> aht pahg·nah·<u>nah</u>·kahw
– a rape	**– ang isáng pánggagahasà** ahng ee·<u>sahng</u> pahng·gah·gah·<u>hah</u>·sah'
– a theft	**– ang isáng pagnanákaw** ahng ee·<u>sahng</u> pahg·nah·<u>nah</u>·kahw
I was *mugged/ robbed*.	**Akó ay *binugbóg/ninakáwan.*** ah·<u>koh</u> ahy bee·noohg·<u>bohg</u>/nee·nah·<u>kah</u>·wahn
I lost my…	**Nawalán akó ng…** nah·wah·<u>lahn</u> ah·<u>koh</u> nahng…
My…was stolen.	**Nanákaw ang…ko.** nah·<u>nah</u>·kahw ahng…koh
– backpack	**– báckpack** <u>bahk</u>·pahk
– camera	**– kámera** <u>kah</u>·meh·rah
– (rental [hire]) car	**– (niréntang) sasakyán** (nee·<u>rehn</u>·tahng) sah·sahk·<u>yahn</u>
– computer	**– kompyúter** kohm·<u>pyoo</u>·tehr
– credit card	**– crédit card** <u>kreh</u>·deet kahrd
– jewelry	**– aláhas** ah·<u>lah</u>·hahs
– money	**– péra** <u>peh</u>·rah
– passport	**– pasapórte** pah·sah·<u>pohr</u>·teh
– purse [handbag]	**– bag** bahg
– traveler's checks [cheques]	**– mgá tráveler's checks** mah·<u>ngah</u> <u>trah</u>·veh·lehrs chehks
– wallet	**– pitáka** pee·<u>tah</u>·kah
I need a police report.	**Kailángan ko ng repórt ng pulís.** kah·ee·<u>lah</u>·ngahn koh nahng reh·<u>pohrt</u> nahng poo·<u>lees</u>

Health

I'm sick [ill].	**May sakít akó.** mahy sah·<u>keet</u> ah·<u>koh</u>
I need an English-speaking doctor.	**Kailángan ko ng doktór na nagsásalitâ ng Inglés.** kah·ee·<u>lah</u>·ngahn koh nahng dohk·<u>tohr</u> nah nahg·<u>sah</u>·sah·lee·<u>tah</u>' nahng eeng·<u>lehs</u>
It hurts here.	**Masakít díto.** mah·sah·<u>keet</u> dee·toh
I have a stomachache.	**Masakít ang tiyán ko.** mah·sah·<u>keet</u> ahng tee·<u>yahn</u> koh

Finding a Doctor

Can you recommend a *doctor/dentist*?	**Pwéde ba kayóng magrékomendá ng *doktór/dentísta*?** <u>pweh</u>·deh bah kah·<u>yohng</u> mahg·<u>reh</u>·koh·mehn·<u>dah</u> nahng *dohk·<u>tohr</u>/dehn·<u>tees</u>·tah*
Can the doctor come here?	**Pwéde bang pumuntá ang doktór díto?** <u>pweh</u>·deh bahng poo·moon·<u>tah</u> ahng dohk·<u>tohr</u> dee·toh
What are the office hours?	**Anóng óras ang pások sa opisína?** ah·<u>nohng</u> <u>oh</u>·rahs ahng <u>pah</u>·sohk sah oh·pee·<u>see</u>·nah
I'd like an appointment for...	**Gustó kong makipág-appóintment...** goos·<u>toh</u> kohng mah·kee·<u>pahg</u>·ah·<u>pohynt</u>·mehnt...
– today	– **ngayón** ngah·<u>yohn</u>
– tomorrow	– **búkas** <u>boo</u>·kahs
– as soon as possible	– **sa lálong madalíng panahón** sah <u>lah</u>·lohng mah·dah·<u>leeng</u> pah·nah·<u>hohn</u>

| It's urgent. | **Madalían itó.** mah·dah·<u>lee</u>·ahn ee·<u>toh</u> |
| I have an appointment with Doctor… | **Méron akóng appóintment kay Doktór…** <u>meh</u>·rohn ah·<u>kohng</u> ah·<u>pohynt</u>·mehnt kahy dohk·<u>tohr</u>… |

Symptoms

I'm…	**…akó.** ah·<u>koh</u>…
– bleeding	**– Dinudugô** dee·noo·doo·<u>goh</u>'
– constipated	**– Cónstipáted** <u>kohns</u>·tee·<u>pehy</u>·tehd
– dizzy	**– Nahihílo** nah·hee·<u>hee</u>·loh
– nauseous	**– Nasusuká** nah·soo·soo·<u>kah</u>
– vomiting	**– Nagsúsuká** nahg·<u>soo</u>·soo·<u>kah</u>
It hurts here.	**Masakít díto.** mah·sah·<u>keet</u> dee·toh
I have…	**Méron akóng…** <u>meh</u>·rohn ah·<u>kohng</u>…
– an allergic reaction	**– állergy** <u>ah</u>·lehr·jee
– chest pain	**– nararámdamang paninikíp ng dibdíb** nah·rah·<u>rahm</u>·dah·mahng pah·nee·nee·<u>keep</u> nang deeb·<u>deeb</u>
– congestion	**– pagbabará** pahg·bah·bah·<u>rah</u>

I have…	**Méron akóng…** meh·rohn ah·kohng…
– cramps	**– pulíkat** poo·lee·kaht
– diarrhea	**– pagtataé** pahg·tah·tah·eh
– an earache	**– nararárámdamang masakít sa taínga** nah·rah·rahm·dah·mahng mah·sah·keet sah tah·ee·ngah
– a fever	**– lagnát** lahg·naht
– pain	**– nararámdaman na pananakít** nah·rah·rahm·dah·mahn nah pah·nah·nah·keet
– a rash	**– pantál** pahn·tahl
– a sprain	**– pílay** peeh·lahy
– some swelling	**– kónting pamamagâ** kohn·teeng pah·mah·mah·gah'
– a sore throat	**– masakít na lalamúnan** mah·sah·keet nah lah·lah·moo·nahn
– a stomachache	**– sakít ng tiyán** sah·keet nahng tee·yahn
– sunstroke	**– súnstroke** sahn·strohwk
I've been sick [ill] for…days.	**May sakít akó ng…áraw.** mahy sah·keet ah·koh nahng…ah·rahw

▶For numbers, see page 181.

Health Conditions

I'm…	**…akó.** …ah·koh
– anemic	**– Anémik** ah·neh·meek
– asthmatic	**– May hikà** mahy hee·kah'
– diabetic	**– Diyabétik** dee·yah·beh·teek
I'm allergic to antibiotics/penicillin.	**May állergy akó sa *antibiótics/penícillin*.** mahy ah·lehr·jee ah·ko sah *ahn·tee·bah·yoh·teeks/peh·nee·see·leen*

▶For food items, see page 90.

I have…	**Méron akóng…** meh·rohn ah·kohng…
– arthritis	– **arthrítis** ahr·thrahy·tees
– a heart condition	– **sakít sa pusò** sah·keet sah poo·soh'
– high/low blood pressure	– **high/lów** blood préssure *hahy/lohw* blahd preh·shoor
I'm on medication.	**Umíinóm akó ng gamót.** oo·mee·ee·nohm ah·koh nahng gah·moht
I'm on…	**Umíinóm akó ng…** oo·mee·ee·nohm ah·koh nahng…

You May Hear…

Anó ang probléma? ah·noh ahng proh·bleh·mah	What's wrong?
Saán ang masakít? sah·ahn ahng mah·sah·keet	Where does it hurt?
Sumásakít ba díto? soo·mah·sah·keet bah dee·toh	Does it hurt here?
Naggágamót ka ba? nahg·gah·gah·moht kah bah	Are you on medication?
May állergy ka ba sa anumáng bágay? mahy ah·lehr·jee kah bah sah ah·noo·mahng bah·gahy	Are you allergic to anything?
Ibukás nga ang iyóng bibíg. ee·boo·kahs ngah ahng ee·yohng bee·beeg	Open your mouth.
Humingá ng malálim. hoo·mee·ngah nahng mah·lah·leem	Breathe deeply.
Umubó ka please. oo·moo·boh kah plees	Cough please.
Magpatingín ka sa espésyalísta. mahg·pah·tee·ngeen kah sah ehs·peh·shah·lees·tah	See a specialist.
Pumuntá ka sa ospitál. poo·moon·tah kah sah ohs·pee·tahl	Go to the hospital.

Treatment

Do I need *a prescription/ medicine*?	**Kailángan ko ba ng *reséta/gamót*?** kah·ee·lah·ngahn koh bah nahng *reh·seh·tah/ gah·moht*
Can you prescribe a generic drug [unbranded medication]?	**Pwéde ba kayóng magreséta ng genéric na gamót?** pweh·deh bah kah·yohng mahg·reh·seh·tah nahng dyeh·neh·reek nah gah·moht
Where can I buy it?	**Saán ko mabíbili iyón?** sah·ahn koh mah·bee·bee·lee ee·yohn

▶ For dosage instructions, see page 173.

Hospital

Notify my family, please.	**Pakísabíhan ang áking pamílya, please.** pah·kee·sah·bee·hahn ahng ah·keeng pah·meel·yah plees
I'm in pain.	**May nararárámdaman akóng sakít.** mahy nah·rah·rahm·dah·mahn ah·kohng sah·keet
I need a *doctor/nurse*.	**Kailángan ko ng *doktór/nars*.** kah·ee·lah·ngahn koh nahng *dohk·tohr/nahrs*
When are visiting hours?	**Kailán ang mgá óras ng pagbisíta?** kah·ee·lahn ahng mah·ngah oh·rahs nahng pahg·bee·see·tah
I'm visiting…	**Bibisitáhin ko ang…** bee·bee·see·tah·heen koh ahng…

Dentist

Can you fix this denture?	**Pwéde ba ninyóng ayúsin ang pustísong itó?** pweh·deh bah neen·yohng ah·yoo·seen ahng poos·tee·sohng ee·toh

I have...	**Méron akóng...** meh·rohn ah·<u>kohng</u>...
– a broken tooth	– **siráng ngípin** see·<u>rahng</u> <u>ngee</u>·peen
– a lost filling	– **natanggál na pásta** nah·tahng·<u>gahl</u> nah <u>pahs</u>·tah
– a toothache	– **masakít na ngípin** mah·sah·<u>keet</u> nah <u>ngee</u>·peen

Gynecologist

I have *cramps/a vaginal infection.*	**Akó ay *pinupulíkat/may impeksiyón sa áking kaselánan.*** ah·<u>koh</u> ahy pee·noo·poo·<u>lee</u>·kaht/mahy eem·pehk·see·<u>yohn</u> sah <u>ah</u>·keeng kah·seh·<u>lah</u>·nahn
I missed my period.	**Hindî akó dinatnán.** heen·<u>dee</u>' ah·<u>koh</u> dee·naht·<u>nahn</u>
I'm on the Pill.	**Gumagámit akó ng pills.** goo·mah·<u>gah</u>·meet ah·<u>koh</u> nahng peehls
I'm (...months) pregnant.	**Buntís akó (ng...buwán).** boon·<u>tees</u> ah·<u>koh</u> (nahng...boo·<u>wahn</u>)
I'm not pregnant.	**Hindî akó buntís.** heen·<u>dee</u>' ah·<u>koh</u> boon·<u>tees</u>
My last period was...	**Ang hulí kong pagrerégla ay...** ahng hoo·<u>lee</u> kohng pahg·reh·<u>rehg</u>·lah ahy...

Optician

I lost...	**Nawalâ ko...** nah·wah·<u>lah</u>' koh...
– a contact lens	– **ang cóntact lens** ahng <u>kohn</u>·tahk lehns
– my glasses	– **ang áking salamín** ahng <u>ah</u>·keeng sah·lah·<u>meen</u>
– a lens	– **ang isáng lens** ahng ee·<u>sahng</u> lehns

Payment and Insurance

How much?	**Magkáno?** mahg·kah·noh
Can I pay by credit card?	**Pwéde ba akóng magbáyad ng crédit card?** pweh·deh bah ah·kohng mahg·bah·yahd nahng kreh·deet kahrd
I have insurance.	**Méron akóng insúrance.** meh·rohn ah·kohng een·shoo·rahns
I need a receipt for my insurance.	**Kailángan ko ng resíbo pára sa áking insúrance.** kah·ee·lah·ngahn koh nahng reh·see·boh pah·rah sah ah·keeng een·shoo·rahns

Pharmacy [Chemist]

Essential

Where's the pharmacy [chemist]?	**Saán ang botíka?** sah·ahn ahng boh·tee·kah
What time does it *open/close*?	**Anóng óras itó *nagbubukás/nagsasará*?** ah·nohng oh·rahs ee·toh nahg·boo·boo·kahs/ nahg·sah·sah·rah
What would you recommend for...?	**Anó ang inyóng mairerékomendá pára sa...?** ah·noh ahng een·yohng mah·ee·reh·reh·koh·mehn·dah pah·rah sah...
How much do I take?	**Gaáno karámi ang kailángan kong inumín?** gah·ah·noh kah·rah·mee ahng kah·ee·lah·ngahn kohng ee·noo·meen
Can you fill [make up] this prescription?	**Pwéde ba ninyó akóng bigyán ng nása resétang itó?** pweh·deh bah neen·yoh ah·kohng beeg·yahn nahng nah·sah reh·seh·tahng ee·toh
I'm allergic to...	**Állergic akó sa...** ah·lehr·jeek ah·koh sah...

72

You may discover that that medication available by prescription only in the U.S. or U.K. is available over the counter in the Philippines. Mercury Drugstore is the largest pharmacy chain with hundreds of branches nationwide; many are open 24 hours. Selection and supplies are limited in rural areas, so it is best to stock up before you leave the major cities. If you're not sure what you need, pharmacists are usually glad to help.

Dosage Instructions

How much do I take?	**Gaáno karámi ang kailángan kong inumín?** gah·<u>ah</u>·noh kah·<u>rah</u>·mee ahng kah·ee·<u>lah</u>·ngahn kohng ee·noo·<u>meen</u>
How often?	**Gaáno kadalás?** gah·<u>ah</u>·noh kah·dah·<u>lahs</u>
Is it safe for children?	**Safe ba itó pára sa mgá batà?** sehyf bah ee·<u>toh</u> <u>pah</u>·rah sah mah·<u>ngah</u> bah·tah'
I'm taking…	**Umíinóm akó ng…** oo·<u>mee</u>·ee·<u>nohm</u> ah·<u>koh</u> nahng…
Are there side effects?	**May mgá ibáng epékto ba itó?** mahy mah·<u>ngah</u> ee·<u>bahng</u> eh·<u>pehk</u>·toh bah ee·<u>toh</u>

You May See…

ISÁNG/TATLÓNG BÉSES SA ISÁNG ÁRAW	*once/three* times a day
TABLÉTA	tablet
PATÁK	drop
KUTSARÍTA	teaspoon
PAGKATÁPOS/BÁGO/ KASABÁY NG PAGKÁIN	*after/before/with* meals
LULUNÍN NG BUÔ	swallow whole
MAAÁRING MAGDÚLOT NG PAGKAHÍLO	may cause drowsiness
PÁRA SA PANLABÁS NA GÁMIT LÁMANG	for external use only

Health Problems

I need something for…	**Kailángan ko ng pára sa…** kah·ee·<u>lah</u>·ngahn koh nahng <u>pah</u>·rah sah…
– a cold	– **sipón** see·<u>pohn</u>
– a cough	– **ubó** oo·<u>boh</u>
– diarrhea	– **pagtataé** pahg·tah·tah·<u>eh</u>
– insect bites	– **kagát ng insékto** kah·<u>gaht</u> nahng een·<u>sehk</u>·toh
– motion [travel] sickness	– **pagkahílo sa biyáhe** pahg·kah·<u>hee</u>·loh sah bee·<u>yah</u>·heh
– a sore throat	– **masakít na lalamúnan** mah·sah·<u>keet</u> nah lah·lah·<u>moo</u>·nahn
– sunburn	– **súnburn** <u>sahn</u>·behrn
– an upset stomach	– **siráng tiyán** see·<u>rahng</u> tee·<u>yahn</u>

Basic Needs

I'd like…	**Gustó ko ng…** goos·<u>toh</u> koh nahng…
– acetaminophen [paracetamol]	– **paracetamól** pah·rah·seh·tah·<u>mohl</u>
– antiseptic cream	– **antiséptic cream** ahn·tee·<u>sehp</u>·teek kreem
– aspirin	– **áspirín** <u>ahs</u>·pee·<u>reen</u>
– bandages	– **mgá bénda** mah·<u>ngah</u> <u>behn</u>·dah
– a comb	– **sukláy** sook·<u>lahy</u>
– condoms	– **mgá kóndom** mah·<u>ngah</u> <u>kohn</u>·dohm
– contact lens solution	– **cóntact lens solútion** <u>kohn</u>·tahk lehns soh·<u>loo</u>·shohn
– deodorant	– **deódoránt** deh·<u>yoh</u>·doh·<u>rahnt</u>
– a hairbrush	– **háirbrush** <u>hehyr</u>·brash
– ibuprofen	– **ibúprofen** ahy·<u>byoo</u>·proh·fehn
– insect repellent	– **pamprotékta sa kagát ng insékto** pahm·proh·<u>tehk</u>·tah sah kah·<u>gaht</u> nahng een·<u>sehk</u>·toh
– lotion	– **lótion** <u>loh</u>·shohn

– a nail file	**– nail file** <u>nehyl</u> fahyl
– a (disposable) razor	**– pang-áhit (na dispósable)** pahng <u>ah</u>·heet (nah dees·<u>poh</u>·sah·bohl)
– razor blades	**– rázor blades** <u>rehy</u>·zohr blehyds
– sanitary napkins [pads]	**– sanitáry nápkins** sah·nee·<u>tah</u>·ree <u>nahp</u>·keens
– shampoo/ conditioner	**– shámpoo/condítioner** <u>shahm</u>·poo/ kohn·<u>dee</u>·shoh·nehr
– soap	**– sabón** sah·<u>bohn</u>
– sunscreen	**– súnblock** <u>sahn</u>·blahk
– tampons	**– támpons** <u>tahm</u>·pohns
– tissues	**– tíssues** <u>tees</u>·yoos
– toilet paper	**– tóilet páper** <u>tohy</u>·let <u>pehy</u>·pehr
– a toothbrush	**– tóothbrush** <u>tooth</u>·brash
– toothpaste	**– tóothpaste** <u>tooth</u>·pehyst

▶ For baby products, see page 158.

Reference

Grammar

Verbs

Conjugation of Filipino verbs is based on the three aspects of the verb—completed (action that has terminated), incompleted (action still in progress) and contemplated (action not yet started). To conjugate regular verbs, affixes are added to the verb and/or the first consonant and vowel of the verb is repeated.

Some of the commonly used affixes are **–um**, **mag–**, **ma–** and **mang–**. When **–um** is used, it is inserted before the first vowel of the verb; when **ma–**, **mag–** or **mang–** is used, it is inserted at the beginning of the verb. In the completed and incompleted aspects, **ma–, mag–** and **mang–** are changed to **na–, nag–** and **nang–**. The incompleted and contemplated aspects are formed by repeating the first syllable of the root word.

In Filipino, the stem or base (root) form of the verb is different from the infinitive. Both the root and infinitive forms are shown in these examples.

Root Word	Infinitive	Completed	Incompleted	Contemplated
hingî	h**um**ingî (to ask for)	h**um**ingî	h**umí**hingì	**hí**hingì
pasyál	**ma**masyál (to stroll)	**na**masyál	**na**mámasyal	**ma**mámasyal
tanóng	**mag**tanóng (to ask a question)	**nag**tanóng	**nag**tátanong	**mag**tátanong
hirám	**mang**hirám (to borrow)	**nang**hirám	**nang**híhiram	**mang**híhiram

Example:

Humingî akó ng travel brochure. (I asked for a travel brochure.)

Nouns and Articles

There are four noun genders in Filipino: feminine, masculine, common and neuter. Nouns that may be either female or male are common nouns, for example: **estudyante** (student), **guro** (teacher) and **kaibigan** (friend). Those without gender are called neuter.

Below are examples of these nouns.

Feminine	Masculine	Common	Neuter
áte (older sister)	**kúya** (older brother)	**kapatíd** (sibling)	**Mayníla** (Manila)
nínang (godmother)	**nínong** (godfather)	**ináanak** (godson or goddaughter)	**diwà** (thought)
inahín (hen)	**tandáng** (rooster)	**manók** (chicken)	**larô** (game)

Feminine and masculine nouns use the marker **si** (singular) and **siná** (plural). Common and neuter nouns use the marker **ang** (singular) and **ang mga** (plural).

Examples:

Nawawalâ **ang mga** bagáhe námin. (Our bags are missing.)

Si Maria ay isáng tour guide. (Maria is a tour guide.)

Siná Jose at Mario ay umalís. (Jose and Mario left.)

In Filipino, nouns are preceded by markers. A marker functions in the same way as articles in English. It is used to indicate that the noun is a thing, place or person.

	Singular	Plural
Names of things	**ang, ng**	**ang mga, ng mga**
Names of places	**sa**	**sa mga**
Names of people	**si, ni, kay**	**siná, niná, kiná**

Mga is the pluralizer for names of things and places and **siná** for names of persons.

Pronouns

Subject pronouns in Filipino are as follows:

I	**akó**
you	**ikáw**
he/she	**siyá**
it	**itó**
we	**táyo** (including person addressed)
	kamí (excluding person addressed)
you (pl.)	**kayó**
they	**silá**

Word Order

Unlike English, word order in Filipino is generally verb – subject. For example:

Sumábog ang Bulkáng Mayón. (Mayon Volcano erupted. Literally: Erupted the Mayon Volcano.)

Filipinos generally use this pattern, especially in conversation. The subject–verb pattern is used mainly in formal speech, such as in interviews, and in print. In such cases, the verb is preceded by **ay**. For example:

Ang Bulkáng Mayón ay sumábog. (Mayon Volcano erupted.)

Negations

There are four negation words in Filipino: **hindî**, **walâ**, **huwág** and **áyaw**. **Hindî**, sometimes shortened to **di**, is used to negate verbs. It means "no" when used alone and "not" when used in a sentence. **Walâ** indicates non-possession or non-existence. **Huwág** is used to express negative commands. **Áyaw** is to dislike or to refuse. In the verb–subject pattern, these words precede the rest of the sentence, for example:

Hindî/Di ako Pilipíno. (I am not a Filipino.)

Walâ kamíng mga ticket. (We do not have tickets.)

Huwág kang tumawíd sa kálye. (Do not cross the street.)

Áyaw náming umuwî. (We do not want to go home.)

Imperatives

To use the command form, simply exclaim the stem of the verb, for example:

Takbó! (Run!)

Uwî! (Go home!)

Alís! (Go away!)

The infinitive form followed by the appropriate pronoun can also be used to express commands:

Tumakbó ka! (Run!)

Umuwî ka! (Go home!)

Umalís kayo! (Go away!)

Comparative and Superlative

When comparing similar things, add **kasing–** to the beginning of the adjective or adverb. The comparative is formed by placing **mas** (more) before the adjective or adverb. **Pinaká–** (most) is added to the adjective or adverb to form the superlative.

Adjective	Equality	Comparative	Superlative
matangkád (tall)	**kasíng**tangkád (as tall as)	**mas** matangkád (taller)	**pinaká**matangkád (tallest)
matamís (sweet)	**kasíng**tamís (as sweet as)	**mas** matamís (sweeter)	**pinaká**matamís (sweetest)
malamíg (cold)	**kasíng**lamíg (as cold as)	**mas** malamíg (colder)	**pinaká**malamíg (coldest)

Possessive Pronouns

Possessive pronouns in Filipino may be placed before (**ákin**, **iyó**, **kanyá**, **ámin**, **átin**, **inyó** and **kanilá**) or after (**ko**, **mo**, **niyá**, **nátin**, **námin**, **ninyó** and **nilá**) the word modified.

mine	**ákin**
yours (sing.)	**iyó**
his, hers	**kanyá**
ours	**átin** (including person addressed) **ámin** (excluding person addressed)
yours (pl.)	**inyó**
theirs	**kanilá**

Examples:

<u>**Ákin**</u> ang wallet na itó. (This wallet is <u>mine</u>.)

<u>**Ámin**</u> ang mga gámit na itó. (These things are <u>ours</u>.)

<u>**Kanyá**</u> ang mga sapátos na iyón. (Those shoes are <u>his/hers</u>.)

Sa <u>**iyó**</u> ba yan? (Is that <u>yours</u>?)

Possessive Adjectives

A possessive adjective follows the noun it modifies.

my	**ko**
your (sing.)	**mo**

his, her	**niyá**
our	**nátin** (including person addressed)
	námin (excluding person addressed)
your (plural)	**ninyó**
their	**nilá**

Example:

Pwédeng hiramín ang lighter <u>mo</u>? (Can I borrow <u>your</u> lighter?)

Adjectives

Filipino adjectives are placed before or after the word they modify. They may be grouped into simple and **ma–** adjectives. For **ma–** adjectives, the prefix **ma–** is added to a noun to indicate the quality that the noun expresses. For example, **maínit** (hot; **init** means heat); **magandá** (beautiful; **ganda** means beauty).

Simple Adjective	Ma– Adjective
payát (thin)	**maínit** (hot)
bágo (new)	**magandá** (beautiful)

Examples:

<u>**Payát**</u> si Brian. (Brian is <u>thin</u>.)

<u>**Bágo**</u> ang mga bag ko. (My bags are <u>new</u>.)

<u>**Maínit**</u> ang panahón. (The weather is <u>hot</u>.)

<u>**Magandá**</u> ang tanáwin. (The view is <u>beautiful</u>.)

Adverbs

In the verb–subject pattern, Filipino adverbs come after the verb.

They describe how, where or when an action occurred.

Adverbs are usually introduced by **nang**.

Example:

Nagsásalità <u>**nang dáhan-dáhan**</u> ang translator. (The translator is speaking <u>slowly</u>.)

Essential

0	**síro** see·roh	
1	**isá** ee·sah	
2	**dalawá** dah·lah·wah	
3	**tatló** taht·loh	
4	**ápat** ah·paht	
5	**limá** lee·mah	
6	**ánim** ah·neem	
7	**pitó** pee·toh	
8	**waló** wah·loh	
9	**siyám** see·yahm	
10	**sampû** sahm·poo'	
11	**labíng-isá** lah·beeng·ee·sah	
12	**labíndalawá** lah·been·dah·lah·wah	
13	**labíntatló** lah·been·taht·loh	
14	**labíng-ápat** lah·beeng·ah·paht	
15	**labínlimá** lah·been·lee·mah	
16	**labíng-ánim** lah·beeng·ah·neem	
17	**labímpitó** lah·beem·pee·toh	
18	**labíngwaló** lah·beeng·wah·loh	
19	**labínsiyám** lah·been·see·yahm	
20	**dalawampû** dah·lah·wahm·poo'	
21	**dalawampú't isá** dah·lah·wahm·poot ee·sah	
22	**dalawampú't dalawá** dah·lah·wahm·poot dah·lah·wah	
30	**tatlumpû** taht·loom·poo'	

31	**tatlumpú't isá** taht·loom·<u>poot</u> ee·<u>sah</u>
40	**ápatnapû** <u>ah</u>·paht·nah·<u>poo</u>'
50	**limampû** lee·mahm·<u>poo</u>'
60	**ánimnapû** <u>ah</u>·neem·nah·<u>poo</u>'
70	**pitumpû** pee·toom·<u>poo</u>'
80	**walumpû** wah·loom·<u>poo</u>'
90	**siyámnapû** see·<u>yahm</u>·nah·<u>poo</u>'
100	**isándaán** ee·<u>sahn</u>·dah·<u>ahn</u>
101	**isándaán at isá** ee·<u>sahn</u>·dah·<u>ahn</u> aht ee·<u>sah</u>
200	**dalawáng daán** dah·lah·<u>wahng</u> dah·<u>ahn</u>
500	**limáng daán** lee·<u>mahng</u> dah·<u>ahn</u>
1,000	**sanlíbo** sahn·<u>lee</u>·boh
10,000	**sampúng líbo** sahm·<u>poong</u> <u>lee</u>·boh
1,000,000	**isáng milyón** ee·<u>sahng</u> meel·<u>yohn</u>

Ordinal Numbers

first	**úna** <u>oo</u>·nah
second	**pangalawá** pah·ngah·lah·<u>wah</u>
third	**pangatló** pah·ngaht·<u>loh</u>
fourth	**pang-ápat** pahng·<u>ah</u>·paht
fifth	**panlimá** pahn·lee·<u>mah</u>
once	**isáng besés** ee·<u>sahng</u> beh·<u>sehs</u>
twice	**dalawáng besés** dah·lah·<u>wahng</u> beh·<u>sehs</u>
three times	**tatlóng besés** taht·<u>lohng</u> beh·<u>sehs</u>

Time

Essential

What time is it?	**Anóng óras na?** ah·<u>nohng</u> <u>oh</u>·rahs nah
It's noon [midday].	**Tanghalì na.** tahng·<u>hah</u>·lee' nah
At midnight.	**Sa hátinggabí.** sah <u>hah</u>·teeng·gah·<u>bee</u>
From one o'clock to two o'clock.	**Mulâ ala-úna hanggáng alás dos.** moo·<u>lah</u>' ah·lah·<u>oo</u>·nah hahng·<u>gahng</u> ah·<u>lahs</u> dohs
Five after [past] three.	**Limáng minúto makaraán ang alás tres.** lee·<u>mahng</u> mee·<u>noo</u>·toh mah·kah·rah·<u>ahn</u> ahng ah·<u>lahs</u> trehs
A quarter to four.	**Labínlimáng minúto bágo mag-alás kuwátro.** lah·<u>been</u>·lee·<u>mahng</u> mee·<u>noo</u>·toh <u>bah</u>·goh mahg·ah·<u>lahs</u> koo·<u>waht</u>·roh
5:30 *a.m./p.m.*	**alás síngko y médya ng *umága/gabí*** ah·<u>lahs</u> <u>seeng</u>·koh ee·<u>mehd</u>·yah nahng *oo·<u>mah</u>·gah/gah·<u>bee</u>*

Days

Essential

Sunday	**Linggó** leeng·<u>goh</u>
Monday	**Lúnes** <u>loo</u>·nehs
Tuesday	**Martés** mahr·<u>tehs</u>
Wednesday	**Miyérkoles** mee·<u>yehr</u>·koh·lehs
Thursday	**Huwébes** hoo·<u>weh</u>·behs
Friday	**Biyérnes** bee·<u>yehr</u>·nehs
Saturday	**Sábadó** <u>sah</u>·bah·<u>doh</u>

Dates

yesterday	**kahápon**	kah·hah·pohn
today	**ngayón**	ngah·yohn
tomorrow	**búkas**	boo·kahs
day	**áraw**	ah·rahw
week	**linggó**	leeng·goh
month	**buwán**	boo·wahn
year	**taón**	tah·ohn

Months

January	**Enéro**	eh·neh·roh
February	**Pebréro**	pehb·reh·roh
March	**Márso**	mahr·soh
April	**Abríl**	ahb·reel
May	**Máyo**	mah·yoh
June	**Húnyo**	hoon·yoh
July	**Húlyo**	hool·yoh
August	**Agósto**	ah·gohs·toh
September	**Setyémbre**	seht·yehm·breh
October	**Októbre**	ohk·too·breh
November	**Nobyémbre**	nohb·yehm·breh
December	**Disyémbre**	dees·yehm·breh

Seasons

summer	**tag-inít**	tahg·ee·neet
the rainy season	**tag-ulán**	tahg·oo·lahn

Holidays

January 1: New Year's Day, **Bàgong Taón**

Movable: Maundy Thursday, **Huwébes Sánto**

Movable: Good Friday, **Biyérnes Sánto**

Movable: Eid ul Fitr, **Eid ul Fitr**

April 9: Bataan and Corregidor Day, **Araw ng Kagitíngan**

May 1: Labor Day, **Araw ng mgá Manggagawà**

June 12: Independence Day, **Araw ng Kalayáan**

Last Sunday of August: National Heroes Day, **Araw ng mgá Bayáni**

November 1: All Saints' Day, **Araw ng mgá Patáy**

November 30: Bonifacio Day, **Araw ni Bonifacio**

December 25: Christmas Day, **Araw ng Paskó**

December 30: Rizal Day, **Araw ni Rizál**

December 31: New Year's Eve, **Hulíng araw ng taón**

Because the Philippines is a mainly Catholic country, the most important holidays are Christmas, Easter and All Soul's Day. New Year's Day is also widely celebrated, usually with fireworks. Holy Week holidays (Maundy Thursday and Good Friday) move each year based on the Catholic Church's liturgical calendar, but usually take place around March or April. Eid ul Fitr or the feast of breaking the fast of Ramadhan is a national holiday in deference to the Filipino Muslim community. This holiday falls on the tenth month of the Islamic calendar.

Conversion Tables

When you know	Multiply by	To find
ounces	28.3	grams
pounds	0.45	kilograms
inches	2.54	centimeters
feet	0.3	meters
miles	1.61	kilometers
square inches	6.45	sq. centimeters
square feet	0.09	sq. meters
square miles	2.59	sq. kilometers
pints (U.S./Brit)	0.47/0.56	liters
gallons (U.S./Brit)	3.8/4.5	liters
Fahrenheit	5/9, after −32	Centigrade
Centigrade	9/5, then +32	Fahrenheit

Mileage

1 km − 0.62 miles	50 km − 31 miles
5 km − 3.1 miles	100 km − 61 miles
10 km − 6.2 miles	

Measurement

1 gram	**isáng grámo** ee·sahng grah·moh	= 0.035 oz.
1 kilogram (kg)	**isáng kílo** ee·sahng kee·loh	= 2.2 lb
1 liter (l)	**isáng lítro** ee·sahng leet·roh	= 1.06 U.S./ 0.88 Brit. quarts
1 centimeter (cm)	**isáng sentimétro** ee·sahng sehn·tee·meht·roh	= 0.4 inch

1 meter (m)	**isáng métro**	= 3.28 feet
	ee·<u>sahng</u> <u>meht</u>·roh	
1 kilometer (km)	**isáng kilométro**	= 0.62 mile
	ee·<u>sahng</u> kee·loo·<u>meht</u>·roh	

Temperature

-40° C – -40° F	-1° C – 30° F	20° C – 68° F
-30° C – -22° F	0° C – 32° F	25° C – 77° F
-20° C – -4° F	5° C – 41° F	30° C – 86° F
-10° C – 14° F	10° C – 50° F	35° C – 95° F
-5° C – 23° F	15° C – 59° F	

Oven Temperature

100° C – 212° F	177° C – 350° F
121° C – 250° F	204° C – 400° F
149° C – 300° F	260° C – 500° F

Useful Websites

www.tourism.gov.ph
*official website for
tourism in Philippines*

www.philippineairlines.com
*Philippine Airlines (the national
airline of Philippines)*

www.superferry.com.ph
*the leading sea transport
of the Philippines*

www.tsa.gov
*U.S. Transportation Security
Administration (TSA)*

www.gov.ph
*official government portal
of the Philippines*

www.mmda.gov.ph
*official website of nation's capital
region of governance and urban
development*

www.lrta.gov.ph
Metro Manila LRT (Light Rail) website

www.caa.co.uk
*U.K. Civil Aviation Authority
(CAA)*

English–Filipino Dictionary

A

accept *v* tanggáp

access *n* daánan

accident aksidénte

acetaminophen paracétamol

acupuncture acupúncture

adapter adápter

address adrés

advance *v* bumále

after paglampás

afternoon hápon

aftershave áftersháve

agency ágency

airline airline

airplane eropláno

airport paliparan

alcohol álkohol

allergic állergic

allow *v* payág

allowed pinapayágan

alone mag-isá

alter bagúhin

alternate ibá

aluminum alúminum

amazing kahanga-hángà

ambulance ambulánsya

amount halagá

amusement amúsement

anemic anémik

animal háyop

another ibá

antibiotic antibiótic

antique antík

antiseptic antiséptic

anything anumán

apartment apártment

appointment appóintment

arcade arcáde

area area

aromatherapy arómathérapy

around sa may

arrivals (airport) pagdatíng

arrive *v* dumatíng

arthritis arthrítis

artificial artifícial

aspirin áspirín

ATM ATM

adj	adjective	BE	British English	n	noun
v	verb				

attraction atraksyón
audio aúdio
authentic awténtikó
automatic automátic
available bakánte

B

baby báby
backpack báckpack
bag súpot
baggage bagáhe
bakery panadérya
ballet ballét
bandage bénda
bank bángko
bar bar
barber barbéro
baseball béysbol
basket básket
basketball básketból
bathroom bányo
battery bateryá
battleground pináglabánan
be ba
beach beach
beautiful magandá
bed káma

bed sheets kúbre káma
before bágo
behind likód
beige beige
belt sinturón
bet pustá
bicycle bisikléta
big malakí
bike bisikléta
bikini bikíni
bill n bill; [BE] (restaurant)
  check
bite n kagát; v kagatín
black itím
bland matabáng
blanket kúmot
bleed dinudugô
blood dugô
blouse blúsa
blue asúl
board v sakáy
boarding sumakáy
boat boat
book book
bookstore boókstore
boot n bóta
boring nakákainíp

botanical botánical

bother *n* abála

bottle bóte

bottle opener pambukás ng bóte

bowl mangkók

box *n* kahón

boxing bóksing

bra bra

bracelet pulséras

breakfast almusál

breathe *v* humingá

bridge tuláy

brief (underpants) brief

broken sirâ

brooch brótse

broom walís

brother kapatíd

brown brown

bug súrot

bus bus

bus station estasyón ng bus

business búsiness

button butón

buy *v* bilí

bye bye

C

cabin kábin

cafe café

call *n* tawág; *v* tawágan

calories cálories

camera kámera

camp kámpo

camping kámping

can láta

can opener ábre-láta

cancel kanselahín

car kótse

card kard

carry *v* dadalhín; dalhín

carry-on bitbítin

cart cart

carton kartón

cash péra

cashier kahéra

casino casíno

cathedral katedrál

Catholic Katóliko

cave kuwéba

CD CD

cell phone céllphone

center cénter

certificate sertípiko

chair chair

change *n* magpápalít; *v* palitán; *n* **(money returned)** suklî

charcoal úling

charge *n* charge; *v* singilin

cheap múra

check check

check-in chéck-in

check-out chéck-out

chemist [BE] botíka

cheque [BE] (banking) check

chest dibdíb

child anák

children mga anák

church simbáhan

class class

classical clássical

clean *adj* malínis

cleaner *n* cléaner

cliff bangín

clock orasán

cleaning panlínis

clear clear

close *v* isará

closed *adj* sarádo

closing *n* pagsará

cloth téla

clothing damít

club club

coat amerikána

code code

cold *adj* malamíg; *n* sipón

collect *adj* kolék; *v* colléct

color kúlay

comb sukláy

computer kompyúter

concert cóncert

conditioner conditioner

condo kóndo

condom kóndom

confirm *v* confirm

connect *v* makakákonék

constipated constipáted

consulate konsuládo

contact *n* kóntak; *v* kóntakin

control kontról

convention convéntion

cook *v* lutò

cooker [BE] kalán

cooking *n* paglulutò

cool mahángin

copper tansô

corkscrew córkscrew

corner kánto

correction corréction

cot fólding bed

cotton kóton

cough *v* umubó; *n* ubó

counter cóunter

country cóuntry

course course

courts courts

cover *n* cóver; *v* takíp

cramps pulíkat
cream kréma
credit krédit
crib krib
cue cue
crystal kristál
cup tása
customs cústoms
cut cut

D

damage *n* sirà
damaged nasirà
dance sayàw
day áraw
debit débit
deck deck
declaration déclarátion
declare *v* deklará
declined *v* tangihán
deep malálim
delay deláy
delete burahín
delicatessen délicatéssen
delicious saráp
denim maóng
dentist dentísta

denture pustíso
deodorant deódoránt
department depártment
departure depárture
deposit *n* depósito; *v* idepósitó
detergent sabóng panlabá
diabetes diabétes
diabetic may diabétes
diamond diyamánte
diarrhea pagtatáé
diesel díesel
difficult mahírap
digital dígital
dine *v* kumáin
direct dirétsong
directory direktóryo
dirty madumí
disconnect *v* diskonek
discount diskwénto
dish *n* pinggán
dishwasher díshwasher
dishwashing liquid sabóng
  panlínis ng pinggán
display case estánte
disposable dispósable
distilled distílled
disturb *v* istórbuhin

dive sísid

divorced diborsyádo

dizzy hílo

doctor doktór

doll manikà

domestic doméstik

domestic flights biyáheng doméstik

door pintô

dress bestída

drink *n* inúm; *v* uminóm

drinking water túbig inúmin

drive *n* maného

drop *n* paták; *v* patakán

dry cleaner dry cleaner

during hábang

duty túngkulin

DVD DVD

E

ear taínga

earrings híkaw

east east

easy madalî

eat *v* kaínin

effect epékto

electric koryénte

elevator élevator

e-mail é-mail

embassy émbaháda

enamel enámel

end *n* tapós; *v* magtapós

English Inglés

engrave ukítan

entrance pasukán

equipment gámit

escalator éscalator

e-ticket e-tícket

evening gabí

exact eksákto

excess sóbra

exchange *n* pálitan; *v* (money) magpapalit

excursion ékskursiyón

exhausted pagód

excuse me pakiúlit namán

exit *n* éxit; labásan; *v* labás

expecting inaasáhan

expensive mahál

express ekspres

extension ékstensiyón

extra ékstra

eyebrow kílay

eyeglasses salamín

F

facial fácial
facility pasilidád
family pamílya
fan béntiladór
far malayò
fare pamasáhe
farm búkid
fast *adj* bilís
father tátay
fax fax
feed *v* pakaínin
ferry férry
fever lagnát
field párang
Filipino Filipíno
fill *v* punuín
fill out sagután
film [BE] pelíkulá
fine mabúti
fire sunóg
first úna
fit kásya
fix ayúsin
flat [BE] apártment
flight lipád
flip-flops tsinélas

fold itupî
food pagkáin
football [BE] sóccer
for pára
forest gúbat
forecast pagtáya ng panahón
fork tinidór
fountain fóuntain
freezer fréezer
fresh sariwà
friend kaibígan; kasáma
from gáling
frying pan kawalì
full punuín
full-service full-sérvice

G

game larô
garbage basúra
garden gárden
gas gas
gas station gásolinahán
generic genéric
get *v* kumúha
get off *v* bababâ
give *v* bigáy
give way magbigáy-daán

glass báso

gluten glútin

go v pumuntá

go out v lumabás

gold gintô

golf golf

good magandá

good afternoon magandáng hápon

good evening magandáng gabí

good morning magandáng umága

grandchild apó

gray abó

green bérde

grocery grócery

groundcloth sapíng panlátag

groundsheet [BE] sapíng panlátag

guide gabáy

gym gym

H

hair buhók

half adj kaláháting

half kilo kaláháting kílo

hammer martílyo

handicapped may kapansánan

hat sombréro

have v makúha

health kalusúgan

heart pusò

heater héater

heel takóng

hello helló

helmet hélmet

help n túlong; v tulúngan

herb yérba

here díto

hero bayáni

hill buról

hire [BE] n rentá; v magrénta

hockey hóckey

holiday [BE] bakasyón

home báhay

hospital ospitál

hostel hóstel

hot maínit

hot water maínit na túbig

hotel hotél

hour óras

housekeeping tagalínis

how paáno

how many pára sa ilán

how much magkáno
how old iláng taón
hug n yákap; v yákapin
hurt adj masakít
husband asáwa

I

I akó
ibuprofen ibúprofen
ice yélo
imported impórted
infection impeksiyón
information ímpormasyón
initial n inisyal; v inisyalán
innocent inosénte
insect insékto
inside loób
inspection ínspeksyón
instant ínstant
insurance insúrance
interest ínteres
interested adj interesádo
interesting interesánte
international internásyonal
international flights
  biyáheng internásyonal
internet ínternet
internet cafe ínternet café

interpreter intérpreter
intersection ínterséksyon
introduce v ipakilála
iron plántsa
itemized bill nakadetálye na bill

J

jacket jácket
jaw pangá
jeans pantalóng maóng
jeepney dyip
jewelry aláhas
join samáhan
jumper [BE] sweáter
junction [BE] ínterséksyon

K

keep (remain) manatíli
key susì
kilo kílo
kilometer kilométro
kiss v halikán
knife kutsílyo

L

lactose intolerant dî pwédeng
  may gátas
lake lawà

lamp lámpara
large malakí
later mamayá
laundrette [BE] palabáhan
laundromat palabáhan
laundry service tagalabá
lawyer abogádo
leather leather
leave (behind) iwánan;
  (go) umalís
left (direction) kaliwâ
less kumúlang
letter súlat
library library
lifeguard lífeguard
lightbulb bombílya
light ilaw
like gustó
line línya
linen línen
liquor álak
list n listáhan
liter lítro
liver atáy
local lokál
lock kandádo
long adj mahabà; (time) tagál

look n itsúra
loose maluwáng
lose mawalâ
love mahál
LRT station estasyón ng LRT
luggage bagáhe

M

machine machíne
magazine mágasín
magnificent magnípico
mail n súlat
main pángunáhin
man laláki
manager mánager
manicure mánicure
manual mánual
map mápa
market paléngke
married may asáwa
mass mísa
massage masáhe
matches pósporó
mean v íbig sabíhin
medication gamót
medium médium
meet (someone) magkíta

meeting méeting
membership mémbership
memory mémory
memorial libíngan
menstrual period régla
menu menú
message mensáhe
midnight hátinggabí
minute minúto
mistake malî
mobile phone [BE] céllphone
money péra
month buwán
more (amount) humigít
more slowly bagálan
morning umága
mosque móske
mother nánay
motorcycle motorsíklo
mountain bundók
mouth bibíg
movie pelíkulá
MRT station estasyón ng MRT
mug v bugbugín
museum muséo
music músika
must kailángan
my ákin

N

name pangálan
napkin nápkin
nationality nasyonalidád
nature kalikásan
nature preserve
  protektádong kalikásan
near malápít
necklace kwintás
new bágo
newspaper dyáryo
next sunód
no (disapproval,
  dislike) áyaw;
  (negative) hindî;
  (prohibited) báwal
no entry báwal pumások
no parking báwal pumárada
no U-turn báwal mag-U-turn
north north
note [BE] n bill
nothing walâ
now ngayón
number númeró

O

office opisína
official offícial

often madalás
OK OK
old lúma
open búksan
opera ópera
opposite kabilâ
orange (color) órange
outlet óutlet
outside sa labás
overnight magdamág

P

pack *n* pakéte; *v* empáke
package pakéte
pajamas pajáma
palace palásyo
pants pantalón
pantyhose pántyhose
paper papél
paracetamol [BE] paracetamól
park *n* párke; *v* pumaráda
passenger pasahéro
passport pasapórte
password pássword
past lumampás
path daánan
pay *v* bayáran; magbáyad

peach (color) peach
peak tuktók
pearls pérlas
pediatrician pediatrícian
pedicure pédicure
peg *n* sípit
pen (for writing) bállpen
penicillin penícillin
per báwat
period (of time) panahón
peso píso
petrol [BE] gas
petrol [BE] station gásolinahán
pewter péwter
pharmacy botíka
Philippines Philippines
phone teléponó
phonecard phónecard
photo retráto
picnic píknik
piece piráso
pillow únan
pink pink
plan pláno
plastic plástik
plate pláto
platinum plátinúm

play (theater) dulâ
plunger pambómba ng inodóro
pole póste
police pulís
pond pond
post [BE] *n* súlat
pot kaldéro
pottery bangá
pregnant buntís
premium prémium
prepaid prépaid
prescription reséta
press pindutín
price présyo
print iprint
private prívate
problem probléma
program prográma
Protestant Protestánte
pull hátak
purple púrple
purpose dahilán
purse bag
push túlak

Q

quiet tahímik
queue [BE] línya

R

racetrack kareráhan
racket rakéta
railway station [BE]
  estasyón ng tren
raincoat kapóte
rainforest rainfórest
rash pantál
razor pang-áhit
real túnay
receipt resíbo
recommend rékomendá
recycle i-recýcle
red pulá
refund refúnd
refrigerator réfrigerátor
region rehiyón
rent *n* rentá; *v* magrénta
repeat ulítin
repellent pamprotékta
report *v* i-repórt; *n* repórt
reservation resérbasyón
reserve resérba
resort resórt
restaurant réstorán
restroom cómfort room (CR)
retired retirádo

return bumalík

right kánan

ring singsíng

ring up [BE] *n* tawág;
  v tawágan

river ílog

road daán

romantic romántiko

room kuwárto

route rúta

rowboat bangká

rubbish [BE] basúra

rugby rúgby

rush madalî

S

same parého

sandal sandályas

sauna sauna

save isáve

scarf bandána

scissors guntíng

sea dágat

security seguridád

see makíta

seaside [BE] beach

self-service self-sérvice

sell itindá

separated hiwaláy

service sérvice

ship ipadalá

shoes sapátos

shop [BE] tindáhan

short (length) maiklî

shorts (clothing) *n* shorts

should dápat

shoulder balíkat

show iturò

shrine shrine

sightseeing sightseeing

sign pirmahán

silk séda

silver sílver

single binatà

sister kapatíd

sit umupô

skirt pálda

slice hiwà

slippers tsinélas

slow bagál

small maliít

sneakers rúbber shoes

soap sabón

soccer sóccer

socks médyas

some kónti

sorry sóri

south south

souvenir soúvenír

spa spa

sparkling spárkling

spatula espátula

speak v mag-úsap;
  (a language) n salitâ

special espesyál

specialist espésyalísta

spell ispél

spoon kutsára

sprain pílay

stadium stádium

stamp (postage) sélyo; v tatak

start n simulâ; v magsimulâ

station estasyón

steep matarík

stolen nákaw

stomach tiyán

stop (vehicles) hintô;
  (people) n tígil; v tumígil

store tindáhan

stove kalán

strange kakaibá

stream bátis

student estudyánte

study mag-áral

stunning kagilá

suit suit

suitable bágay

suitcase maléta

sunglasses súnglasses

sunny maáraw

super súper

supermarket súpermárket

supply gámit

swallow lulunín

sweater sweáter

sweatshirt swéatshirt

sweet sweet

swelling pamamagâ

swimsuit swímsuit

symbol símbolo

synagogue sýnagogue

T

table mésa

tablet tabléta

tail buntót

take (get) kumuha;
  (fetch) kunín

take away [BE] take out

take off hubarín

tank tanké

tap grípo

202

taste tikmán

taxi táksi

teaspoon kutsaríta

temple témplo

tennis ténnis

tent tént

tent peg sípit ng tent

terminal términál

terrible nápakasamâ

thank you salámat

that iyán

theater teátro

there doón

thing gámit

think isípin

this itó

throat lalamúnan

ticket tíket

tie kurbáta

tight masikíp

tights [BE] pántyhose

time óras

tin [BE] láta

to sa

to go (food) take out

tobacco tabáko

today ngayón

together magkásáma

toilet [BE] cómfort room (CR)

toilet paper tísyu

tomorrow búkas

tongue dilà

tonight ngayóng gabí

too (excess) masyádo

tooth ngípin

toothbrush toothbrush

toothpaste toothpaste

total lahát

tough matigás

tour tour

tourist turísta

towel tuwálya

town báyan

town center plása

toy laruán

traffic tráffic

trails daánan

train tren

train station estasyón ng tren

translate isálin

trash basúra

travel trável

traveler tráveler

treatment treatment

tricycle (motorcycle with sidecar) tráysikél

trip biyáhe
trolley trólley
trousers [BE] pantalón
T-shirt T-shirt
turn on buksán
TV TV
type itype

U

U.K. U.K.
U.S. U.S.
ugly pángit
umbrella páyong
understand intíndihin
underwear únderwear
unemployed waláng trabáho
username úsername
utensil gámit

V

vacation bakasyón
valley lambák
value halagá
vegetarian végetárian
visit bumisíta
volleyball vólleyból
vomit suká

W

wait hintáy
waiter wéyter
waitress wéytres
wake (someone up) gisíngin
walk lakád
wallet pitáka
warm v inítin; adj maínit
watch reló
water túbig
waterfall talón
way daán
we kamí
weather panahón
week linggó
west west
what anó
wheelchair wheelchair
when kailán
where saán
which alín
white putî
who síno
whole buô
widowed biyúdo
wife asáwa

204

window bintanà
wine list listáhan ng álak
wireless wíreless
with kasabáy
woman babáe
wool lána
work trabáho
wrap *v* balútin; *n* pambálot
write ísúlat

Y

year taón
yellow diláw
yes óo

Z

zoo zoo

Filipino-English Dictionary

A

abála *n* bother
abaláhin *v* bother
abogádo lawyer
abó gray
ábre-láta can opener
acupúncture acupuncture
adápter adapter
adrés address
áftersháve aftershave
ágency agency
ákin my
akó I
aksidénte accident
aláhas jewelry
álak liquor
alín which
álkohol alcohol
allérgic allergic
almusál breakfast
alúminum aluminum
ambulánsya ambulance
amerikána coat
amúsement amusement
anák child

anémik anemic
anó what
antibiótic antibiotic
antík antique
antiséptic antiseptic
anumán anything
apártment apartment [flat BE]
apó grandchild
apóy *n* fire (flame)
apple apple
appóintment appointment
áraw day
arcáde arcade
area area
arómathérapy aromatherapy
arthrítis arthritis
artifícial artificial
asáwa husband; wife
áspirín aspirin
asúl blue
atáy liver
ATM ATM
atraksyón attraction
aúdio audio
automátic automatic
awténtikó authentic
áyaw no (disapproval, dislike)
ayúsin *v* fix

B

ba be
babáe woman
báby baby
báckpack backpack
bag purse
bagáhe luggage
bagál slow
bágay suitable
bágo before; new
bagúhin alter
báhay home
bakánte available
bakasyón vacation [holiday BE]
balíkat shoulder
ballét ballet
ballpen pen (for writing)
balútin v wrap
bandána scarf
bangá pottery
bangín cliff
bangká rowboat
bángko bank
bányo bathroom [toilet BE]
bar bar
barbéro barber
baryá n change (coins)

básket basket
básketból basketball
báso glass
basúra garbage [rubbish BE]
batà child
bàtis stream
bateryá battery
báwal no (prohibited)
báwal mag-U-turn no U-turn
báwal pumárada no parking
báwal pumások no entry
báwat per
báyan town
bayáni hero
bayáran pay
beach beach [seaside BE]
beige beige
bénda bandage
béntiladór fan (appliance)
bérde green
bestída dress
béysbol baseball
bibíg mouth
bikíni bikini
bill n bill [note BE]
binatà single
bintanà window
bisikléta bicycle

bitbítin carry-on
[hand luggage BE]

biyáhe trip

biyáheng doméstik
domestic flights

biyáheng internásyonal
international flights

biyúdo widowed

blúsa blouse

boat boat

bóksing boxing

bombílya lightbulb

book book

boókstore bookstore

bóta *n* boot

botánical botanical

bóte bottle

botíka pharmacy [chemist BE]

bra bra

brief brief (underpants)

brótse brooch

brown brown

bugbugín *v* mug

buhók hair

búkas tomorrow

búkid farm

búksan open

buksán turn on

bumabâ *v* get off

bumále *v* advance

bumalík return

bumilí *v* buy

bumisíta visit

bundók mountain

buntís pregnant

buntót tail

buô whole

burahín *v* delete

buról hill

bus bus

búsiness business

butón button

buwán month

bye bye

C

café cafe

cálories calories

cart cart

casíno casino

CD CD

céllphone cell phone
[mobile phone BE]

cénter center

céreal cereal

chair chair

charge *n* charge

check check [cheque BE] (banking)

chéck-in check-in

chéck-out check-out

Christmas Christmas

class class

clássical classical

cleaner *n* cleaner

clear *n* clear

club club

code code

cómfort room (CR) restroom [toilet BE]

cóncert concert

condítioner conditioner

constípated constipated

convéntion convention

córkscrew corkscrew

corréction correction

cóunter counter

country country

course course

courts courts

cue cue

cup cup

cústoms customs

daán road; way

daánan *n* access; path; trails

dágat sea

dahilán purpose

dalhín *v* carry

damít clothing

dápat should

dárating arrive

débit debit

deck deck

déclarátion declaration

deláy delay

délicatéssen delicatessen

dentísta dentist

deódoránt deodorant

depártment department

depárture departure

depósitó *n* deposit

dî pwédeng may gátas lactose intolerant

diabétes diabetes

dibdíb chest

diborsyádo divorced

díesel diesel

dígital digital

dilà tongue
diláw yellow
dinudugô bleeding
direktóryo directory
dirétso direct
díshwasher dishwasher
diskonek *v* disconnect
diskwénto discount
dispósable disposable
distílled distilled
díto here
diyamánte diamond
doktór doctor
dóllars dollars
doméstik domestic
doón there
dry cleaner dry cleaner
dugô blood
dulâ play (theater)
dumatíng *v* arrive
DVD DVD
dyáryo newspaper
dyip jeepney

E

east east
eksákto *adj* exact
ékskursiyón excursion

ékspres express
ékstensiyón extension
ékstra extra
élevator elevator
é-mail e-mail
émbaháda embassy
enámel enamel
empáke pack
epékto effect
eropláno airplane
éscalator escalator
espátula spatula
espesyál special
espésyalísta specialist
estánte display case
estasyón station
estasyón ng bus bus station
estasyón ng LRT LRT station
estasyón ng MRT MRT station
estasyón ng tren train
 [railway BE] station
estudyánte student
e-tícket e-ticket
éxit exit [way out BE]

F

fácial facial
fax fax

férry ferry
Filipíno Filipino
fountain fountain
fréezer freezer
full-sérvice full-service

G

gabáy guide
gabí evening
gáling from
gámit equipment; supplies; thing; utensil
gamítin bágo best if used by
gamót medication
gárden garden
gas gas [petrol BE]
gásolinahán gas [petrol BE] station
genéric generic
gin gin
gintô gold
gisíngin wake (someone up)
glútin gluten
golf golf
grípo tap
grócery grocery
gúbat forest
gúlay vegetable

guntíng scissors
gustó like
gym gym

H

hábang during
halagá amount; value
halikán v kiss
hápon afternoon
hátak pull
hátinggabí midnight
háyop animal
héater heater
hélmet helmet
híkaw earrings
hílo dizzy
hindî no (negative)
hintáy wait
hintô stop (vehicles)
hiwà n slice; cut
hiwáin v cut
hiwaláy separated
hóckey hockey
hóstel hostel
hotél hotel
hubarín take off
humigít more (amount)
humingá v breathe

ibá alternate; another

íbig sabíhin mean

ibigáy v give

ibúprofen ibuprofen

ideklará v declare

idepósitó v deposit

ispél spell

ilaw light

ílog river

impeksiyón infection

ímpormasyón information

impórted imported

inaasáhan expecting

Inglés English

inidóro toilet

iníhaw barbecue

inísyal n initial

inisyalán v initial

inítin v warm

inosénte innocent

insékto insect

ínspeksyón inspection

ínstant instant

insúrance insurance

ínteres interest

interesádo adj interested

interesánte interesting

internásyonal international

ínternet internet

intérpreter interpreter

ínterséksyon intersection [junction BE]

intíndihin understand

inúmin n drink

ipadalá ship

ipakilála v introduce

iprínt print

i-recýcle recycle

i-repórt report

isálin translate

isará v close

isáve save

isdâ fish

isípin think

istórbuhin v disturb

isúlat write

itím black

itindá sell

itindá bágo sell by

itó this

itsúra n look

itupî v fold

iturò show

itype type

iwánan leave (behind)
iyán that

J

jácket jacket

K

kabilâ opposite
kábin cabin
kagát *n* bite
kagatín *v* bite
kagilá stunning
kahanga-hangà amazing
kahéra cashier
kahón *n* box
kaibígan friend
kailán when
kailángan must
kaínin *v* eat
kakaibá strange
kalaháti *adj* half
kalaháting kílo half-kilo
kalán stove [cooker BE]
kaldéro pot
kalikásan nature
kaliwâ left (direction)
kalusugán health
káma bed

kámera camera
kamí we
kámping camping
kámpo camp
kánan right
kandádo lock
kanselahín cancel
kánto corner
kapatíd brother; sister
kapóte raincoat
kard card
kareráhan racetrack
kartón carton
kasabáy with
kasáma friend
kásya fit
katedrál cathedral
katapusán *n* end
Katóliko Catholic
kawalì frying pan
kílay eyebrow
kílo kilo
kilómetro kilometer
kinúha take
kolék *adj* collect (phone call)
kompyúter computer
kóndo condo
kóndom condom

konék *v* connect
konsuládo consulate
kóntak *n* contact
kóntakin *v* contact
kónti some
kontról control
koryénte electric
kóton cotton
kótse car
krédit credit
krib crib
kristál crystal
kúbre káma bed sheets
kúlay color
kúnin take (fetch)
kurbáta tie
kumáin *v* dine
kúmot blanket
kumpirmahín *v* confirm
kumúha *v* take (get)
kumúlang less
kutsára spoon
kutsaríta teaspoon
kutsílyo knife
kuwárto room
kuwéba cave
kwintás necklace

labás *v* exit
labásan *n* exit
lagnát fever
lahát total
lakád walk
laláki man
lalamúnan throat
lambák valley
lámpara lamp
lána wool
larô game
laruán toy
láta can [tin BE]
lawà lake
léather leather
libíngan memorial
library library
lífeguard lifeguard
likód behind
línen linen
linggó week
linísin *v* clean
línya line [queue BE]
lipád flight
listáhan *n* list

listáhan ng álak wine list
lítro liter
lokál local
loób inside
lúma old
lulunín swallow
lumabás v exit; go out
lutúin v cook

M

maáraw sunny
mabilís adj fast
mabúti fine
machíne machine
madalás often
madalî easy; rush
madumí dirty
magandá beautiful; good
mag-áral study
mágasin magazine
magbáyad v pay
magbigáy-daán give way
magdamág overnight
mag-isá alone
magkásáma together
magkáno how much
magkíta meet (someone)

magmaného v drive
magnípiko magnificent
magpapalít v change (foreign exchange); exchange (money)
magréta v rent [hire BE]
magsimulâ start
mahabà long
mahál expensive
magtapós end
mahál love
mahángin cool (temperature)
mahírap difficult
maiklî short
maínit hot (temperature)
mag-úsap talk
makíta see
malakí big
malálim deep
malamíg adj cold
malápít near
malayò far
maléta suitcase
malî mistake
maliít small
maluwáng loose
malínis adj clean
mamayâ later

mánager manager
manatíli keep (remain)
mangkók bowl
mangulékta v collect (things)
maniká doll
mánicure manicure
mánual manual
máong denim
mápa map
martílyo hammer
masáhe massage
masakít adj hurt
masaráp delicious
masikíp tight
masyádo too (excess)
matabâ adj fat
matabáng bland
matarík steep
matigás tough
maulán rainy
mawalâ lose
may asáwa married
may diabétes diabetic
may kapansánan handicapped
médium medium
médyas socks
méeting meeting

mémbership membership
mémory memory
mensáhe message
menú menu
meron v have
mésa table
mga apó grandchildren
mga batà children
minúto minute
mísa mass
móske mosque
motorsíklo motorcycle
mulâ from
múra cheap
muséo museum
músika music

N

nakákainíp boring
nakadetálye itemized
nákaw stolen
nánay mother
nápakasamâ terrible
nápkin napkin
nasirà damaged
nasyonalidád nationality
ngayón now; today

ngayóng gabí tonight
ngípin tooth
north north
número number

O

offícial official
ókey OK
óo yes
ópera opera
opisína office
órange orange
óras hour; time
orasán clock
ospitál hospital
óutlet outlet

P

paáno how
pagkáin food
paglampás after
paglulutò cooking
pagód exhausted
pagsará *n* closing
pagtataé diarrhea
pagtáya ng panahón forecast
pajáma pajamas

pakaínin *v* feed
pakéte package; pack
palabáhan laundromat
[laundrette BE]
palásyo palace
pálda skirt
palipáran airport
palitán *n* change (foreign exchange)
pálitan *n* exchange
paléngke market
pamamagâ swelling
pamasáhe fare
pambálot *n* wrap
pambómba ng inodóro plunger
pambukás ng bóte bottle opener
pamílya family
pamprotékta repellent
panadérya bakery
panahón period (of time); weather
pangá jaw
pang-áhit razor
pangálan name
pángit ugly
pángunahín main
panlínis cleaning

pantál rash
pantalón pants [trousers BE]
pantalóng maóng jeans
pántyhose pantyhose [tights BE]
papaalís departures (airport)
papél paper
pára for
paracétamol acetaminophen
párang field
paratíng arrivals (airport)
parého same
párke *n* park
pasahéro passenger
pasapórte passport
pasilidád facilities
pássword password
pasukán entrance
paták *n* drop
patakán *v* drop
payágan *v* allow
páyong umbrella
pediatrícian pediatrician
pédicure pedicure
pelikulá movie [film BE]
penícillin penicillin
péra cash; money
pérlas pearls

péwter pewter
Philippines Philippines
phónecard phonecard
píknik picnic
pílay sprain
pináglabánan battleground
pinapayágan allowed
pindutín press
pinggán dishes (plates)
pink pink
pintô door
piráso piece
pirmahán sign
píso peso (Filipino currency)
pitáka wallet
pláno plan
plántsa iron
plása town center
plástik plastic
plátinúm platinum
pláto plate
pond pond
pósporó matches
póste pole
prémium premium
prépaid prepaid
présyo price

prívate private

probléma problem

prográma program

protektádong kalikásan nature preserve

Protestánte Protestant

pulá red

pulíkat cramps

pulís police

pumaráda v park

pumuntá v go

punô full

punuín v fill

pulséras bracelet

púrple purple

pusò heart

pustá bet

pustíso denture

putáhe dishes (food)

putî white

R

rainfórest rainforest

rakéta racket

réfrigerátor refrigerator

refúnd refund

régla menstrual period

rehiyón region

rékomendá recommend

reló watch

rentá rent [hire BE]

repórt report

resérba reserve

resérbasyón reservation

reséta prescription

resíbo receipt

resórt resort

réstorán restaurant

retirádo retired

retráto photo

romántiko romantic

rúbber shoes sneakers

rúgby rugby

rúta route

S

sa to

sa labás outside

sa may around

saán where

sabón soap

sabóng panlabá detergent

sabóng panlínis ng pinggán dishwashing liquid

sagután fill out

salámat thank you

salamín eyeglasses

salitâ speak (a language)

samáhan join

sandályas sandal

sapátos shoes

sapíng panlátag groundcloth

sarádo *adj* closed

sariwà fresh (food)

sauna sauna

sayáw dance

séda silk

seguridád security

self-sérvice self-service

sélyo stamp (postage)

sertípiko certificate

sérvice service

shorts *n* shorts (clothing)

shrine shrine

sightseeing sightseeing

sílver silver

simbáhan church

símbolo symbol

simulâ *n* start

singilín *v* charge

singsíng ring

síno who

sinturón belt

sípit *n* peg

sípit ng tent tent peg

sipón *n* cold (sickness)

sirà *n* damage

sirâ broken

sísid dive

sóbra excess

sóccer soccer [football BE]

sombréro hat

sóri sorry

south south

soúvenir souvenir

spa spa

spárkling sparkling

stádium stadium

start start

suit suit

suká vomit

sukláy comb

suklî *n* change (money returned)

súlat letter; *n* mail [post BE]

sumakáy *v* board

sumásakáy boarding

súnglasses sunglasses

sunód next

súnog *n* fire

súper super

súpermárket supermárket

súpot bag

súrot bug

susì key

sweáter sweater [jumper BE]

swéatshirt sweatshirt

sweet sweet

swímsuit swimsuit
  [swimming costumes BE]

sýnagogue synagogue

T

tabáko tobacco

tabléta tablet

tagál long (time)

tagalabá laundry service

tagalínis housekeeping (hotel)

taga-lúto *n* cook

tahímik quiet

taínga ear

take out to go [take away BE]

takóng heel

takíp *n* cover

takpán *v* cover

táksi taxi

talón waterfall

tanggáp *v* accept

tanggihán declined

tanké tank

tansô copper

taón year

tápos end

tapúsin *v* end

tása cup

taták *v* stamp

tátay father

táwag *n* call

tawágan *v* call

teátro theater

téla cloth

teléponó phone

témplo temple

ténnis tennis

términál terminal

tígil stop (people)

tihéras cot

tíket ticket

tikmán taste

tindáhan store [shop BE]

tinidór fork

tísyu toilet paper

tiyán stomach

toothbrush toothbrush
toothpaste toothpaste
tour tour
trabáho work
tráffic traffic
trável travel
tráveler traveler
tráysikél tricycle (motorcycle with a sidecar)
treatment treatment
tren train
trólley trolley
T-shirt T-shirt
tsinélas flip-flops; slippers
túbig water
túbig inúmin drinking water
tuktók peak
túlak push
tuláy bridge
túlong *n* help
tulúngan *v* help
tumáwag *v* call
tumútulóy staying
túnay real
túngkulin duty
turísta tourist
tuwálya towel
TV TV

U.K. U.K.
U.S. U.S.
ikítan engrave
ubó *n* cough
úling charcoal
ulítin repeat
umága morning
umalís leave (go)
uminóm *v* drink
umubó *v* cough
umupô sit
úna first
únan pillow
únderwear underwear
úsername username

végetárian vegetarian
vólleyból volleyball

walâ nothing
walís broom
west west
wéyter waiter
wéytres waitress

wheelchair wheelchair
wíreless wireless

Y

yákap *n* hug
yakápin *v* hug
yélo ice
yérba herb

Z

zoo zoo